DATE DUE

	MAY 0 6 1996	MAY 1 7 1996	

THE SLAVE TRADE TODAY

THE
SLAVE TRADE
TODAY

By
SEAN O'CALLAGHAN

CROWN PUBLISHERS, INC.   ·   NEW YORK

Printed in the U.S.A.

CONTENTS

Foreword

SOME PEOPLE WILL disbelieve this book. They will say it is the work of a writer with a vivid imagination, but no facts. Others will ask how it was possible to secure the information contained in its pages, how and why did people talk so freely to an Englishman. The truth is that although coming from the British Isles, I am not an Englishman, and do not travel on a British passport. I own a publishing firm in British East Africa, as well as being an author, and visit the countries mentioned in this book in connection with my business as a publisher of travel books. Although, like most other people, I knew that slaves were held in Saudi Arabia and the Yemen, where slavery is still legal, I had no idea of its existence or ramifications in Africa until I met Andrew B. and commenced my investigations. It will be asked why I did not use proper names in this book. The reason is simple. Men like Andrew B. would lose their jobs immediately. While I believe that General Abboud has gone all out in an effort to clean up corrupt officialdom in the Sudan, and strike at the root of the evil protection of the slavers, the Sudanese are a proud people, and as a young nation do not like the world to know that such evil existed in their midst. Consequently Andrew B. and other Europeans who supplied me with information might be asked to resign from the good jobs they hold. Again it might be asked why I do not give the names of the slavers, the Ethiopian, the Egyptian, etc. Again the reason is simple. My living lies in these countries, and life is cheap there. I have given De Jong's true name, because he is dead, and have given Carl von Berg's true name because I would like to see him dead, as I believe Europeans who enter this filthy trade are lower than the lowest native procurer.

I am often asked what could be done to stop this traffic in human souls. The answer is nothing, while America is pouring billions of dollars each year into Saudi Arabia in oil royalties. Stop that, and the trade would stop. It is a matter of simple economics. A young virgin girl costs eight hundred pounds, a boy six hundred pounds, a Cadillac three thousand five hundred pounds. Most rich Saudis have three or four Cadillacs, and as a man's prestige in Saudi Arabia depends on the number of slaves he holds, each rich oil sheikh has at least fifty or sixty human beings in bondage. Deny them the money to buy either cars or human beings and the bottom will fall out of the slave market. It will be argued that slavery has always existed in Saudi Arabia. I agree. In the old days when supervision by nations was impossible and when the slave trade flourished freely, the price of a young girl stood at around fifty pounds. Today no slaver would risk his neck or his liberty for such a paltry sum. Destroy the source of income, and the Ethiopian, the Egyptian, Big Mama, The Fat One, and Carl von Berg will quickly go out of business. Unfortunately in the greedy power-mad world that is ours today, this is not likely to happen.

THE AUTHOR

PART I

MY OWN EXPERIENCE

Chapter I

AT FIRST SIGHT it looked like an ordinary camel train. Through our binoculars we watched it approach the wadi. Two scouts rode ahead, serviceable-looking rifles held at the ready across their knees. Seven of the camels comprising the main train were double loaded. The three luggage animals were piled high with the necessities for a long desert journey.

As it drew nearer we noticed other things. No camel bells tinkled in the clear morning air. The camels looked tired, as if they had been driven hard all night. The whole train had a furtive air, although it was well away from the nearest caravan trails, and three hundred miles from the nearest habitation, in the wild unmapped desert of northern Darfur, in the Sudan. They had need for secrecy, those human vultures who rode this camel trail, for its cargo was flesh and blood, contraband flesh, destined for the port of Suakin; human flesh which would fetch a high price in the markets of the Yemen or Saudi Arabia.

I had first heard of these caravans, bearing their burdens of human misery, in Khartoum in 1957. All the information about them was second-hand, somebody always knew somebody who had seen them, but there was no direct evidence that they existed. Government sources in Khartoum refused to discuss the subject, although one police official admitted that the previous year a combined police and army patrol had pushed far into the northern desert, almost to the Egyptian border, in the hope of catching slavers who were reported to be operating in that area.

Thus, while second-hand rumour was rife in Khartoum, a conspiracy of silence seemed to exist in Government circles.

It was then that I met Andrew B. He was employed as an engineer by the Department of Roads and Communications of the Sudan Government and travelled thousands of miles each year, building roads and bridges. One evening in the bar of the Grand Hotel in Khartoum the talk turned to the old slave roads from the South to Suakin. Andrew B. mentioned that in his last construction job in the Kordofan Province he laid a stretch of road along the old slave-trading route. While the work was in progress they unearthed skulls and bones of the miserable wretches who perished on the long trek from the South to the seaboard.

"It's a strange feeling," Andrew remarked, "unearthing the remains of slaves by day, and at night hearing the cries of people being taken to be sold in the slave markets of Saudi Arabia and the Yemen."

I looked at him in astonishment. At first I thought he was joking. I had heard so many tall tales of present-day slavery in that very bar that I was frankly sceptical. But he was deadly serious.

"You probably won't believe it," he said, "but it is absolutely true. Lying in my tent at night I have heard the caravans passing, and the screams and cries keep me awake for hours afterwards."

"But, good God, man," I said "what do you do about it?"

"Do?" he answered bitterly. "What is there to do about it? Twice I reported it to my chief, here in Khartoum. The first time he passed my report on to the Chief of Police. No action was taken, at least, none that I ever heard about. The second time I got a gentle hint that it might be wiser if I minded my own business. Don't misunderstand me," he continued, "I don't suggest for a moment that the Sudanese Government are implicated in it, or are anything but desperately worried by it, but they do not like the outside world to know about it. They think the Sudan's prestige abroad will suffer, and so are trying to fight it single-handed."

"And you," I asked, "what are you doing about it?"

"Nothing," Andrew answered, "simply nothing; there is nothing I can do."

Later, sitting on the veranda, watching the Nile flow sluggishly by, he gave me further details, details he had picked up in five years work in the remote provinces of Darfur, Kordofan, Bahrel Ghazal, and Equatoria. As a construction engineer he often spent up to ten months in these provinces, the only white man in charge of a construction team of two to three hundred natives.

His methods of operation were as follows. He left Khartoum with a nucleus of skilled men, tractor drivers, bulldozer operators, maintenance men, etc. Arriving at the site of the proposed road or bridge he recruited labour locally, paying the nearest village chief for the labour he supplied. In many cases the "labourers" were girls and young women, dressed in nothing but a G-string. Andrew spoke Arabic fluently and was liked and respected by the chiefs and workers.

He first learned of the slave traders from the chief of a village near Tambura, close to the French Equatorial and Belgian Congo borders. A few days before he arrived there a slave caravan had passed, coming from the direction of the Belgian Congo. The chief's son, out late one night, had heard the mysterious caravan approaching. From a hiding place he had watched it pass, ten swift racing camels with two baggage animals. The chief's son later swore that one of the party was a white man, although this could never be confirmed. It was evident that they were highly organised. Later several caravans passed that way, as it was evidently a recognised route for bringing slaves from the Congo.

Andrew first saw a slave caravan about a year later, when he was constructing a road in Darfur. He had camped near a small oasis, and late that night he heard a camel train approach. Thinking that the visitors had been delayed by the sandstorm which had sprung up that day, he paid it no further attention and crawled into his tent. Next morning he was up at daybreak, as was his custom. The visitors of the previous night had gone, and there was no sign that they had camped there. His foreman, seeing him examine the camel tracks whispered the one word "Abto" (slaves), a word which still strikes terror into the heart of the southern Negro. On his return to Khartoum he reported the matter to his superior, but heard no more about it.

His second encounter with slavers almost cost him his life. This time it took place in Kordofan, about a hundred miles north of Sodiri. One evening he was riding in a jeep in advance of his main column of tractors and bulldozers. Night falls swiftly in Sudan, and he was searching for a suitable camping place. Topping a small ridge, he saw in the depression below him an encampment of about twenty camels. They had evidently been there all day as equipment was scattered around. Two goat's-hair tents had been erected to give shelter from the sun. The look-outs, who had been dozing, went into action immediately. Bullets whistled around the jeep, and only the quick thinking of his driver in turning the jeep around and gaining the shelter of the ridge saved their lives. Andrew carried a .45 Webley revolver for his personal protection, the only arms allowed his column, but he realised it was useless against the modern rifles of the slavers. He returned to his outfit, and spent the night in the open. It was when he reported this incident that he was told it would be wiser if he minded his own business.

In the years that followed he had heard the slave trains passing many times, but was always careful to avoid a head-on encounter. The slavers were as anxious as he was to avoid one. They travel at night, lying up during the day at some hidden water hole or isolated oasis, with look-outs posted, to avoid surprise. They travel in small parties, carrying from twelve to twenty slaves, with three or four guards.

Such was the camel caravan we saw coming towards us on that June morning in 1958 in Darfur. Through our binoculars we could see that it consisted of three guards, Arabs to judge by their features, and fourteen negro slaves, riding two to a camel. The old days of a slave caravan of perhaps a hundred to two hundred slaves are gone for ever.

As they halted at the oasis, the camels knelt, grunting. One of the "points" rode back to the main body, leaving his companion as look-out. As the slaves were helped off the camels we could see through the binoculars that each two were chained together by a thin chain attached to collars round their necks. Ten were girls and four were boys, whose ages seemed to range between ten and eighteen or twenty. When they had all dismounted they were lined up and a guard fastened what seemed to be a long thin chain to the collar of each of them, binding them all together. This left their hands free, but effectively prevented any attempt at escape. Where one went all had to go, even to relieving the wants of nature.

A goat's-hair lean-to was pitched and the captives were hurried into it. We saw the guards take a bag, presumably containing food, from the baggage camel, and hurry into the lean-to. No fire was lit, as the smoke in the thin clear air might attract unwelcome attention. A second guard came from the lean-to and mounted a camel. He rode slowly towards the ridge where we were hidden. It was time to go. A .45 revolver is a poor defence against a service rifle.

Chapter II

I RETURNED FROM Darbur to Khartoum determined to do what Andrew, because of his official position, had been unable to do. I could not get out of my mind the picture of those girls and boys chained together, and I knew that I would not rest until I had tracked down and exposed those evil men who were the brains behind the whole loathsome business of slavery in the Sudan.

I called first at the Ministry of Information, only to be told that the Minister was too busy to see me. However, I managed to see a senior official, who was an Englishman.

When I told him my business, he threw up his hands in horror. "It's ridiculous, my dear Mr. John," he said. "I'm afraid you've been listening to a lot of rubbish that's talked in the bars in Khartoum."

I felt my hackles rising. "It isn't a question of hearsay. I've seen one of these slave trains," I insisted.

"You must have been mistaken. This is 1958 and not 1858." The senior official's smile suggested that I might possibly have suffered a touch of the sun. "The Sudanese are civilised people, and they would never allow anything like that to happen in their country."

"Isn't it possible that the Government doesn't know what's going on in some of the more remote parts of their territory?" I said.

The senior official brushed aside such a possibility. "I would remind you that in the Sudan today there is a highly trained and organised police force and army—a legacy from the days when we ruled here," he added archly.

"The country is so vast—" I began.

"Each province has its own Governor," he pointed out, cutting me short. "And there are army and police posts everywhere."

But I was determined not to be put off. "Have you ever been in Northern Darfur, say, two hundred miles beyond Mellit?"

"I must confess that I have not," he admitted with reluctance.

"Isn't it just possible that a hundred slave trains could hide out in an area such as that without notice?" I insisted.

The senior official's neck reddened. "I've no idea what you're driving at, Mr. John. But I must advise you to be careful. Journalists are not popular with the Government, particularly when they try to pry into affairs which are none of their business," he added. Then he turned to his Sudanese clerk and ordered him to show me out.

Once outside the door, the clerk said in good English: "I could not help overhearing what you were discussing, sir. Mr. X is not correct. There is slavery in the Sudan."

I looked at him with surprise. "How do you know?"

"I know a woman in Omdurman who keeps a house where young girls are bought and sold, sir," he answered frankly.

"Does Mr. X know of this place?" I asked.

"I attempted to tell him once, sir," he replied naïvely, "but I was warned that if I valued my job I had better never speak of it again."

"Where is this place? Could you take me to it?" I asked with a growing sense of excitement.

For a second, I thought I detected a flicker of fear in the fellow's eyes.

"I would have to be very careful, sir. If it became known that you intended to write about the slave trade, your life and mine would be in danger. The Nile does not reveal its secrets," he added in an ominous whisper.

"When can you arrange to take me there?" I asked, refusing to be frightened.

"I will contact you at your hotel, sir," the clerk answered glancing over his shoulder at Mr. X's office door. And with that promise I had to be content, for it was obvious that the man went in fear of the senior official.

I spent the next three days in a state of suspense. A dozen times I asked the manager if there had been any telephone calls for me, only to be told politely that there had been none. My impatience was not eased by the fact that Mr. X and his wife were staying in the hotel, and as often as we met in the bar he would make facetious remarks about the slave trade. In the end, I pretended to be no longer interested.

"It looks as though you were right," I flattered. "Apparently, there is nothing in these stories."

X rose like a fat trout. "I'm glad you've found our Ministry of Information is of some use after all, if it is only to give the lie to all these damn-fool rumours," he laughed.

Three days later, his clerk telephoned to arrange our rendezvous, naming a native bar at which Europeans sometimes drank.

I met him at eight o'clock that evening. He introduced me to another Sudanese, who he said would take me to the house in Omdurman. I was to be introduced as a representative of a firm which had branches all over Africa and the Middle East. I was assured that Europeans employed by the firm often went to the house to buy slave girls before being transferred from Khartoum to the provinces. Posing as one of them, I could look the girls over and then reject them on one pretext or another. After that, we could explain to the woman who managed the house the type of girl I wanted. The clerk added that I would have to pay twenty-five Sudanese pounds as security.

I immediately became suspicious, for the whole transaction seemed little more than a clumsy trap to rob me of twenty-five pounds. While I was more than willing to pay that sum to prove that slavery existed in the Sudan, I was not prepared to lose it through a confidence trick played by two astute local civil servants. Nevertheless, if I let this opportunity slip there was the risk that another chance might not come my way.

Both men were watching me closely.

"Is it agreed, sir?" the clerk asked politely.

I nodded my head, and he spoke rapidly to his companion. Although my Arabic is by no means fluent, I was able to catch the gist of what he said. "Take care that no harm befalls him." Such instructions could mean anything or nothing, I reflected, as I drained my glass of native beer.

Omdurman is an unsavoury place at any time, and after dark white men avoid it. It was for that very reason that I had decided to bring my own taxi driver with me. Mahomed was a villainous-looking cut-throat who drove me whenever I was in Khartoum, and with the exception of Andrew was about the only man I trusted in the whole of the Sudan. He didn't understand a word of English, but before leaving the hotel I had managed to explain to him where I was going that night. He had grinned at me and pulling up the sleeve of his galabeyah patted the long knife strapped to his arm above the elbow. Its blade gleamed in the moonlight, and I recognised it as one of those razor-sharp knives used by the native crocodile hunters. Its haft could be easily reached through the loose neck of his galabeyah.

My friend the clerk had protested at Mahomed's presence, but when I made it clear that I had no intention of going to Omdurman without my bodyguard, he shrugged his shoulders and said: "As you wish, sir."

Now, as I climbed into the taxi accompanied by the clerk's Sudanese friend I was more than ever glad that Mahomed was with us.

Once we had reached the junction of the Blue and White Niles and passed the Mahdi's tomb, to turn into the labyrinth of narrow alley-ways in the *suk*, I thanked all the stars in the indigo sky for the long knife Mahomed was carrying. When, finally, we came to an alley-way too narrow for the car, we pulled up and the Sudanese whispered that it would be wiser to leave the driver behind. But Mahomed was already at my heels as we picked our way through the piles of garbage and stinking pools of urine.

When we arrived at a low door set in the mud wall, the Sudanese knocked twice and then three times. I heard shuffling footsteps across the inner courtyard and a husky voice called: "Shoe buddak?" ("Who is it?") Our guide answered in a whisper. Then the door opened wide enough to allow us to squeeze through one at a time, and was slammed and bolted behind us.

I found myself in a wide courtyard, its walls flanked by rope beds. A shaft of light fell across the broken stone paving, and I saw standing in the doorway immediately opposite an enormously fat woman. Her shadow cast by the light of the room seemed to reach out at me like a giant octopus, so that I recoiled instinctively.

With a huge arm hanging with sagging flesh she waved us into the room. As my eyes grew accustomed to the light, I saw that its floor was spread with fine Persian rugs, and other rugs and tapestries hung from the walls. At one end a beautifully carved screen half-hid a doorway leading to an inner room.

The fat woman lowered herself on to a divan and sat staring up at me, her vast breasts heaving, so that she reminded me no longer of an octopus but a great repulsive toad. The Sudanese introduced me and explained that since I spoke no Arabic, he would act as my interpreter. I was, he said, a newly arrived member of Messrs. B.Z. & Co.

I saw her heavy-lidded eyes light up at the mention of the name, and she gave me a leering smile.

"He wants a girl for his house," the Sudanese said.

"Ask him what type of girl he wants."

The Sudanese translated her question.

"Tell her that I haven't made up my mind. Tell her I would like to see what she has to offer."

I saw her give me a shrewd glance, and the Sudanese must have seen it too, for he hastened to explain that as a newcomer to Africa I had never had a native girl before.

Apparently satisfied, she leaned back on the low divan while we drank our three welcoming cups of sickly sweet coffee in silence. When we had finished, she clapped her podgy beringed hands, and the screen was drawn aside.

A young girl glided silently into the room. I stared at her in amazement. She could not have been more than fourteen years old, and but for the pale duskiness of her skin, with her blue eyes and fair hair reaching to her shoulder, she could have been English. She was naked to the waist, her breasts bare. And as she came timidly towards us, she tried to cover them with her hands. But as the fat woman croaked at her in Arabic, her hands dropped to her sides.

"Tell him I will take five hundred Sudanese pounds for her. Tell him she is the daughter of an English officer and an Arab girl. Tell him I could sell her for twice that sum in Saudi Arabia to the King himself, if I could transport her there. Tell him it is only because she is so nearly white that I cannot take such a risk and so I am prepared to sell her cheaply here."

I could scarcely believe that the old baggage was talking about the lovely child standing demurely in front of me.

Unable to speak, I shook my head. The fat woman rasped out some order to the girl. For a second, the child hesitated and I heard her utter a little gasp that was almost a sob. Then with trembling fingers she fumbled with the fastening of her long white skirt. As it fell to the floor about her ankles, she stepped out of it and stood stark naked before me.

"Tell her I can't afford five hundred pounds," I said, hardly recognising the sound of my own voice.

The fat woman waved the frightened child roughly away. "Ask him what he can afford," she demanded.

"One hundred is my limit," I told the Sudanese.

As he repeated this sum in her ear, her great face reddened under its coating of white powder and she pounded the divan with her huge fist, the spittle drooling from the corners of her flabby mouth. From the little I could understand of her Arabic, I gathered that she was upbraiding the Sudanese for bringing a beggar to her establishment. And the more he tried to pacify her, the more she screamed at him.

"Tell the pig I have only two girls at that price in my house. One is a Sudanese bitch of thirteen, the other a scraggy Arab hen of eleven. The Arab is a virgin," she added slyly.

Then she clapped her hands again, and once more the screen was drawn aside.

The Sudanese girl came first. She was big and well-developed for her age. Her kinky hair was heavily oiled, and she grinned at us boldly, showing her strong white teeth.

Without waiting for the fat woman's orders she dropped her skirt and walked towards me, swaying her buttocks provocatively. Her skin was the colour of a black grape and gleamed in the lamplight. Her pointed nipples were rouged scarlet.

As I again shook my head, she turned and walked sulkily out of the room.

Then, the Arab girl came in. She was little more than a child and so pitifully thin that her tiny breasts were barely formed. As she let fall her skirt, I stifled a gasp of horror, for I saw the angry red weals of lash-marks across her buttocks.

"Send her away!" I shouted.

The fat woman let out a shrill scream of rage.

"Ask the fat pig what he wants. Me!" she shrieked.

The Sudanese tried to quieten her. "He wants a grown girl; a girl of about twenty."

"A girl of twenty?" The heavy-lidded eyes of the old vulture glared at me with contempt. "Does he not know that in the East a girl of twenty is already an old woman? I haven't such a creature in my house. Perhaps, he would like instead a young boy," she jeered. "But if he wants a twenty-year-old I will find him one by next week if he pays me twenty-five pounds deposit now," she added holding out a predatory hand.

I opened my wallet and counted out the notes. All I wanted was to get out of the place, and once outside in the darkness of the courtyard, I leaned against the wall and struggled not to be sick.

Chapter III

I LAY BACK in the taxi and closed my eyes. Not nine miles from Khartoum, the capital of the Sudan, a country which is a member of the United Nations Organisation, the buying and selling of slaves was still a flourishing and profitable business. That night, at a price, I could have bought a lovely fourteen-year-old girl with blue eyes and golden hair for less money and with considerably less fuss than a good second-hand car.

As if reading my thoughts, the Sudanese said with a smile: "Do you believe us now, sir?"

"Why do you ask?" I queried.

"In the beerhouse you were uncertain. You thought, did you not, that we told you about this house simply to rob you of your twenty-five pounds?" he suggested.

"Frankly, yes," I admitted. "But now I'm convinced. What I can't understand is how this can go on more or less openly in the capital of a country which claims to be civilised. Why don't the police do something about it?"

"It is better, sir, not to talk about the police," the Sudanese whispered.

"But, why? For God's sake, why?" I cried.

"Because of this." He made the age-old gesture of rubbing his thumb and forefinger together. "If you take my advice you will never speak of what you have just seen to the police."

"How do you come to be mixed up in all this?" I asked with a sudden feeling of revulsion for him.

He shrugged his shoulders, spreading his hands. "I am only a guide, sir. Sometimes, I work for the Information Office—

23

sometimes not. My friend told me that you are interested in slaves and that you would pay well if I took you to Madame's establishment. The commission is small, but one must make one's living as best one can," he added apologetically.

"Who pays you your commission?"

"The fat one. She gives me ten per cent on every girl she sells through me," the Sudanese answered.

"Does she sell many?"

"Not many. There is no great demand for them in Khartoum now, except among the white men working for B.Z. & Company. Some of them buy girls to take with them for comfort when they are sent to lonely places. But often they prefer boys," he added without disgust. "The commission is small, for boys are cheaper."

"But you said she usually keeps twelve or fourteen girls in her house."

"Most of them will be sent to Saudi Arabia or the Yemen. She buys them locally or from the desert tribes who are too poor to keep them. Then she sells them to the Egyptian," the Sudanese explained.

"Who do you mean by the Egyptian?" I asked with interest.

"The Egyptian who is staying in your hotel," the Sudanese answered lowering his voice to a whisper. "He pretends that he is a cotton buyer. But his real business is buying slaves—young girls and boys—for shipment across the Red Sea."

"But doesn't the Government know about this?" I asked incredulously.

Again, the Sudanese shrugged his shoulders. "Who am I, sir, to say what the Government knows? All I know is that the Egyptian is a good friend of a senior police officer. And since they have become friends, the police officer has bought himself a grand new house in Ga'ama Avenue and a 1958 Oldsmobile convertible. Even a senior police officer does not earn enough to live in such a manner," he added with a touch of envy.

"Do you mean to say Mr. X knows nothing of this?"

The Sudanese laughed softly. "I do not think he knows anything, but I am sure he suspects. Like everyone else in the Sudan he discourages interest in the matter for fear of losing his job."

"Tell me about this Egyptian?" I asked. "Do you mean that he is behind all the slave traffic in the Sudan?"

"That I cannot say. I do not believe that he has anything to do with the caravans bringing slaves from the Belgian Congo or French Equatorial Africa. I only know that he is friendly with the traders and arranges for them to take some of the girls he buys from the fat one down to the coast. It is my opinion that the Egyptian is more concerned with the brothels for they are a safer and more profitable business," the Sudanese said shrewdly.

I had noticed the Egyptian in the Grand Hotel. Not that there was anything particularly remarkable about him, but at that time when relations between Egypt and the Sudan were strained, one could not fail to notice the presence of an Egyptian, particularly a prosperous-looking one, in Khartoum. And the little fat man who smelt so strongly of scent and who always wore a well-pressed suit, even on the hottest days, was so obviously prosperous.

I remembered that he always carried a splendid pig-skin brief-case with glinting gold locks, smoked expensive cigarettes, and was often the centre of a little coterie of acquaintances at a table in a corner of the bar. They were a bizarre collection; a sly-looking Frenchman with a patch over one eye; an Englishman called George, fat, sweating and noisy, who claimed to be an oil prospector; several shady-looking Sudanese, and usually a couple of suave, bespectacled Saudi Arabians. Because he was English, I had made a few discreet inquiries about George. But not even the manager seemed to know anything about him, even to his discredit. More often than not, he was accompanied by a friend, a swarthy Greek or Armenian, who was reputed to own a gold mine in the Red Sea hills, which he apparently ran while drinking absinthe in the Grand Hotel Bar.

Unprepossessing though they were, I determined to become acquainted with the little group of friends. And a few days later, I was given the chance I was looking for when George walked in to the bar. Beyond the fact that he had an inexhaustible supply of dirty stories and that the pockets of his crumpled linen suit bulged with pornographic photographs, I knew nothing about him. However, I asked him to join me in a drink.

By the time he had come to the point of his latest almost interminable story, we were joined by the Egyptian and an introduction had been effected. Having achieved my objective, I made my excuses and left the party, which by then had grown to a dozen.

That evening while I was sitting on the veranda after dinner, I was both surprised and delighted when the Egyptian joined me. Drawing up a chair, he offered me a cigarette from his magnificent gold case, and then clapped his fat damp little hands for the waiter. For a while as we sipped our coffee, we chatted inconsequently of this and that. Then, he asked me what I did. I knew that he was perfectly aware of my profession, for in Khartoum everyone knows what everyone else is doing. So I answered simply: "I write books."

"I knew that," he said blandly. "But what type of books do you write, Mr. John?"

"Mainly travel books," I told him.

"Do you write for any particular firm or are you what is known as a free-lance?"

"A free-lance."

He studied the ash of his cigarette. "I believe you travel through Djibouti and Aden?" Even in the darkness, I could feel his small dark eyes watching me closely, and I had the uncomfortable feeling that he had made it his business to find out all about me. But it seemed pointless to lie.

"I was there last year, and will have to go there again this year before going on to Nairobi," I said.

I heard his basket chair creak beneath his weight as he moved closer. "Please do not think me impertinent, but do these travel books of yours pay you well?"

Coming from a complete stranger, the question was so personal that I laughed. "I don't make a fortune, if that's what you mean. But I make a living."

The Egyptian gave what might have been either a little grunt of satisfaction or condolence, and then lapsed into silence.

"Mr. John, I will be perfectly frank with you," he said, patting my knee. "I have made certain inquiries about you, and all that I have discovered has been to my satisfaction and your credit."

"Thank you," I said, for I could think of nothing else to say.

"Would you be at all interested, Mr. John, in working for me?"

I was so utterly taken aback, that I just stared at him foolishly.

"I might be interested if I knew what sort of work was expected of me. After all, it isn't every day of the week I'm offered a job by a complete stranger. What's the catch to it?"

The Egyptian made a little clicking noise with his tongue.

"I assure you there is no catch to it, Mr. John," he said archly. "The job is so simple that it will not even interfere with your writing. At the same time, it is quite lucrative. Shall we say, that it would allow you to travel in considerable comfort. Permit me to order a drink for you. A whisky and soda?"

Without waiting for an answer, the Egyptian clapped his hands. When the waiter arrived, he ordered a large whisky and soda for me and fresh lime juice for himself.

"I will be perfectly frank with you," he repeated, relaxing into his chair and stretching his short legs. "As you probably are aware, since the Suez trouble we Egyptians have been unable to visit British or French territories. Now, I have many very important connections in those territories, and since this foolish ban my business has suffered severely. I have endeavoured to do my best by correspondence. But you know, Mr. John, what letter-writing is in the Middle East." He spread his fat, carefully manicured hands. "One writes and writes again. But one never gets a reply. What I need is someone—someone like yourself for example—whom I can trust and who is passing through these territories to visit my clients and deliver certain messages on my behalf. For such a service I would be prepared to pay handsomely, Mr. John."

"What makes you think you can trust me?" I asked.

"I have already told you that I have made certain inquiries about you which have proved satisfactory," the Egyptian smiled.

"Why not your friend George? He's British and doesn't need a visa for French territory."

The Egyptian leaned towards me. "Shall we say that he is not so presentable as yourself," he said ingratiatingly. "Besides he is too busy here in the Sudan," he added, lest, I supposed, like everyone else in Khartoum I might be a bearer of gossip.

A silence fell between us while the Egyptian lit one of his large oval cigarettes.

"Well, Mr. John—are you interested?" he asked, watching me closely. "I am prepared to pay you exactly double the figure you made on your travel book last year, and I will accept your word as to what that figure was."

"Give me a few days to think about it. After all, you've rather sprung all this on me," I said.

"By all means. As you know, I am staying in the hotel. So when you have made up your mind, you have only to tell me," he said, holding out his hand.

The following morning I sought out Andrew and told him exactly what had happened.

"What do you make of it?" I asked, when I had finished my story.

Andrew frowned. "I had a pretty shrewd suspicion that the Egyptian was mixed up in the slave racket. But I didn't think—and I still don't—that he's the big white chief. There's someone here in the Sudan, either in the Government or closely connected with it, who's the boss."

"What about the high police official who's a friend of the Egyptian?" I suggested.

Andrew shook his head and laughed. "I know the fellow. He hasn't the intelligence to run a business of this sort. He's nothing more than a stooge. The man you are looking for has brains—real brains. The trouble is he takes good care never to appear in public."

"But what about this job? Shall I take it?"

"If it simply means you're a courier delivering letters or orders, I should be inclined to take it," Andrew advised. "It'll give you the chance to look into the organisation, and when you're satisfied that you have got enough evidence to hang them, well, go ahead and hang 'em!" he laughed.

"Why do you think he picked on me?" I asked, puzzled.

Andrew reflected for a moment and then grinned. "He probably thought that as an author and being too fond of the booze, you were hard-up and open to offer. The odds are that he decided that you'd be only to glad to earn a bit of extra cash without asking too many questions. And, to be honest, if I were in your shoes, I'd jump at it."

I spent the next two days in a state of indecision and then sought out the Egyptian.

"I've thought over your offer and I've decided to accept it provided that I'm not expected to do anything illegal," I told him.

He contrived to look pleased and shocked at the same time. "I'm delighted, Mr. John," he said. "But I assure you that I would never ask you to do anything illegal." Then, taking me by the arm he led me to his favourite corner of the bar and ordered me a double whisky.

"I must give you some idea of our organisation. I take it you have already been told that I am not a cotton buyer?" he asked with a sly smile.

I said that I had heard rumours to that effect, but had not given them much thought. The Egyptian chuckled. "Khartoum is filled with rumours; some true, others false. But that I am not a cotton buyer happens to be true. Our organisation is concerned chiefly with providing girls for the cabarets and houses of entertainment all over the Middle East. You are not shocked, Mr. John?" he asked almost coyly.

When I said "Not in the least," the Egyptian patted my arm and said that he had been correct in supposing me to be an *homme du monde*.

"All our girls join the organisation of their own free-will," he lied blandly. "In fact, some of them find their work so congenial that they send home for their sisters to join them. I am sure you will understand me when I say that our only real difficulty is in overcoming the tiresome formalities concerning passports. We have our ways and means of transporting the girls from place to place, but there is no need for you to concern yourself with such details. All that concerns you is that at this moment, as I explained the other evening, owing to the unfortunate incident at Suez, I am unable to make personal contact with some of my agents. I cannot trust such business to the mail, you understand. All I want you to do, Mr. John, is to visit these agents for me and deliver into their hands certain written instructions that I will give you."

"And for that you are prepared to pay me the double of what I made out of my last travel book?" I asked.

"That is what I promised you, and I am a man of my word," the Egyptian assured me loftily. "Are you satisfied?"

"Perfectly," I told him. "Altogether my last book brought me in five hundred pounds."

"So little?" he asked, and the note of pity in his voice gave me the courage to add that in addition to my royalties I managed to extract a further two hundred pounds towards my travelling expenses.

"Very well, then, I am willing to pay you double," he told me magnanimously. "You will be paid part of the money by each agent you visit together with the expenses of your journey. The balance will be lodged for you in any bank you choose here in Khartoum at the end of your tour. Does that meet with your satisfaction?"

"Absolutely," I said.

He rubbed his fat little hands together. "And when will you be ready to leave Khartoum?"

"In a week's time I shall be going to Asmara and Addis Ababa and then on to Djibouti," I told him.

"Excellent! In that case, I will give you a letter for each place, including Addis Ababa. Although I am at liberty to go to

Ethiopia, I would prefer not to make the journey. You see, I am anxious to go to El Obeid as soon as possible—to-morrow, in fact, as I have some most important business to transact. However, I will contact you immediately I return." He rose to his feet and putting an arm round my shoulder, led me to the bar. "You must drink to the success of our business association, Mr. John. I am sure neither of us will have cause for regret."

"In lime juice?" I queried as he gave the order.

"If you will excuse me, yes. My vices are few, Mr. John," he twinkled.

When the Egyptian left me, I stayed on at the empty bar. El Obeid, I reflected, was but a hundred and fifty miles south-east of Sodiri, where Andrew was working on a new road. If he happened to be awake tomorrow night, the chances were he would hear another camel train passing his tent.

Chapter IV

I HAD BEEN careful not to lie to the Egyptian about myself. Indeed, since he had made inquiries about me, there would have been little point in doing so. However, one thing worried me. If he or any of his henchmen found out that I had been to the fat woman's house, posing as an employee of B.Z. & Company, I would certainly lose my new job. I determined, therefore, to find the Sudanese who had taken me to Ondurman. I found him in the native bar where we had first met, and the moment he saw me he came over to my table.

I explained why I had come. "If the fat woman spreads the news that I visited her place and that I am employed by B.Z. & Co., I'm sunk," I told him.

"She wouldn't dare say a word to anyone," he assured me.

"What about the Egyptian?" I asked.

He shook his head. "He is the last person she would tell. You see, she is supposed to keep the pick of her girls for him, and I know for certain he has never seen the half-white one she offered to you."

"Then, why did she offer her to me?"

The Sudanese laughed. "Because she thought you would give her a better price, sir. The Egyptian will probably pay two hundred and fifty pounds for the girl, unless some white man buys her. The fat one was speaking the truth when she told you that the girl was difficult to sell because of her light colour. I know several rich Sudanese merchants who would buy her, but they dare not. In the end, she will finish hidden away in some brothel like Maria."

"Who was Maria?" I asked, ordering two more beers.

"She was a beautiful girl of pure Italian blood. Beautiful like a water-lily," the Sudanese said, kissing the tips of his black fingers. "The Egyptian bought her from Big Mama in Asmara. Big Mama, like the fat one, sells girls, but she also runs a whore-house as a side line. If you have time, I will tell you the story of Maria," he suggested swallowing his beer.

"I have plenty of time," I told him, calling to the barman to re-fill his glass.

"Maria was only a little baby at the time of the liberation of Ethiopia. Her parents were Italian peasants who with thousands of others had come to Abyssinia to build Mussolini's colonial empire for him. And like thousands of others, they were mur-dered by the Ethiopians. Papa was castrated and his balls hung up outside some Ethiopian's hut. Mama had her belly slit open after she had been raped. Somehow, the Ethiopians missed the baby Maria and someone sold her to Big Mama." The Sudanese sucked at his beer glass with his thick lips.

"Big Mama was good to the baby and brought her up with her own child—a boy she had called George, after your late King.

"When Maria was about sixteen, the Egyptian came to Big Mama's house to buy girls. He saw Maria and was crazy for her. She was tall and beautiful with lovely dark eyes and long dark hair. The Egyptian asked Mama to sell her to him. But the old woman screamed that she would not sell Maria who was like her own daughter. Every day the Egyptian asked Mama to sell, and every day he raised his price. Then, one day he offered a thousand pounds for the girl, and that was a sum that Big Mama had not the heart to refuse.

"The Egyptian took Maria to Cairo on one of his false pass-ports, and kept her in his apartment for six months. Then, he grew tired of her. So he made plans to send her to Paris where he had many connections with the big-time procurers. But before he could make his arrangements, the Suez war started, and the Egyptian was left with Maria on his hands," the Sudanese laughed.

"What happened?" I asked.

"He dared not put her into a brothel or cabaret in Cairo, because not long before one of his girls had cut her throat, and Nasser's police had asked some awkward questions about her passport. But the Egyptian had spent a lot of money on Maria and he wanted to get it back somehow. He doesn't like making a bad deal, that one! So he got Maria another passport and sent her to Khartoum to Mahmoud's whore-house."

"Where is that?"

"Behind the General Hospital. Mahmoud gave her her own room, instead of making her sleep with all the other girls in the courtyard, who only used the big bedrooms for business. Maria is reserved for Members of Parliament, high Civil Servants, senior Army officers, and those white men who are friends of Mahmoud. She does very well," the Sudanese ended laconically.

It was an incredible story and, frankly, I doubted the truth of it. While I knew the Egyptian was capable of any villainy, I did not believe he would have the nerve to buy a white girl in Asmara and keep her in a brothel in Khartoum. Unless, of course, the transaction had all been arranged with the connivance of his friend in the police or some high official. Nevertheless, although the Sudanese swore that his story was true, I determined to find out for myself.

Mahmoud's brothel was situated about three-quarters of a mile from the centre of Khartoum in a quiet and highly respectable street behind the General Hospital. As it was only a few doors away from the Nurses' Home, it was most conveniently placed for those Europeans who visited it. If their cars were seen in the neighbourhood, they could always make the excuse that they were visiting friends in the Nurses' Home.

Like everyone else, I had heard about Mahmoud, although I had never seen him. I knew that he was a Sudanese-Egyptian half-breed, and had been told that as well as owning the brothel and acting as procurer, he personally entertained clients who had homosexual tendencies. The actual management of the brothel was in the hands of a Sudanese called Madam Wan-ei, who was known locally as "Madam One-eye." She was a martinet who ruled her establishment with an iron discipline and was not above taking her whip to the girls who disobeyed her.

All this I had gleaned from Mahomed, my driver, and from the Sudanese.

At the time I visited Mahmoud's, there were ten girls working there; four Sudanese, three Ethiopians, two Arabs, and one Indian. How the last came to be there, I never discovered, unless she had been brought from Port Sudan where there was a small Indian community.

According to Mahomed, all the girls were virtually slaves, owning nothing of their own, for the very clothes they wore belonged to Mahmoud. In theory, a certain percentage of their earning was set aside for them each week. But since, in addition to the thrashings, Mahmoud had instituted a system of fines for breaches of the rules of the establishment, the girls were always penniless. Thus, they could never hope to save enough money to escape, even if they had been able to climb the high wall, topped by barbed wire, which surrounded the courtyard. Moreover, in case of accidents, Mahmoud employed two huge black thugs whose duty it was to keep the girls in and unwelcome visitors out.

Mahmoud's was a two-storey building surrounded by a courtyard along the walls of which were rows of beds on which the girls sat or lay while waiting for customers. On the ground floor were three bedrooms, all furnished in the same hideous Victorian style. The principal piece of furniture of each was a vast brass bed adorned with a plush cover and pillows with crocheted lace edges. In one room I distinctly remember being astonished by a huge engraving of the Queen-Empress framed in red velvet. In any of them one's great-aunt would have felt perfectly at ease.

It was into one of these frightful rooms that I was ushered by the woman who must have been "Madame One-eye." When she realised that I was English, she called loudly for Mahmoud.

He came mincing down the stairs to greet me, dressed in tight black trousers, white silk shirt, and a scarlet cummerbund.

"Good evening, sir," he lisped in perfect English. "Thank you for visiting us. Who did you say had recommended you?" He sounded so exactly like the manageress of a respectable English pension in Mentone that I wanted to laugh.

"I didn't say," I told him. "But for your information, I'm a friend of the Egyptian."

The effect was magical. "I'm honoured to have you, sir," he said. "You must come upstairs. These rooms are for ordinary visitors," he explained, waving a slender hand with varnished nails towards the ground floor.

I followed his swaying buttocks up the stairs and into a room furnished with almost oriental splendour which gave on to a balcony on which there was a large divan spread with Persian rugs.

Mahmoud crossed to a lovely inlaid table and picked up a bottle of Haig.

"This is a special occasion, sir. I hope you will come often now that you know where we are." He poured out two generous drinks. "Cheery O!" he simpered.

When we had finished our drinks, he turned to business. "And now for your pleasure, sir," he said. "I pride myself that I, Mahmoud, can offer you any type of entertainment you desire. My girls are the finest in Africa. Let me show you their photographs. Just pick the one you fancy, and I will have her sent up here immediately."

As I glanced through the photographs, which left nothing to the imagination, Mahmoud watched me closely. As I handed them back to him, he asked: "Which one would you like, sir?"

"None of them," I told him.

For a moment, his face fell. Then, he looked at me through his mascarraed lashes, running a red tongue over his lips.

"I think I understand. Perhaps you will do me the honour of permitting me to entertain you?"

I felt sick.

"Listen, Mahmoud," I said, "if I am to be entertained tonight it will be by Maria."

At the mention of the name he nearly let fall the glass he was holding, and I swear that his dark skin paled. "Maria! Who told you about Maria?" he asked.

"You must remember that I am a friend of the Egyptian," I said.

For a moment he hesitated. Then, he said. "She is very expensive, sir. I charge five pounds for a short time with Maria. If you spend the night with her it will cost you twenty pounds."

"Very well, Mahmoud," I said firmly "I shall spend a short time with her. So please fetch her for me."

With a certain reluctance he went downstairs, and as I helped myself to some more of his Haig, I heard him calling to "Madam One-eye."

After a few minutes he returned, followed by Maria. To say that she was beautiful would be an understatement. She couldn't have been more than seventeen years old, and she was one of the most ravishing creatures I have ever set eyes on. Her skin was the colour of ivory and her black hair hung loosely over her shoulders. Beneath their long dark lashes her eyes were the colour of aquamarines. She was wearing a flowing black chiffon dressing-gown, caught up under her full young breasts with a jewelled brooch, that did little more than veil her nakedness.

"She doesn't speak English, sir," Mahmoud told me, "but she has learned Arabic quickly."

When we were alone together, I spoke to Maria in Italian, half-hoping that she might still remember her native tongue. But she stared at me without understanding. So I was forced to resort to my indifferent Arabic. Since I soon discovered that Maria's was not much more fluent, our conversation was somewhat stilted. However, with the aid of signs, I managed to confirm that the story the Sudanese had told me was true.

So far as her life in Mahmoud's establishment was concerned, Maria appeared to have few complaints, except that the other girls shunned her. When I asked if she liked her life, she shrugged her lovely shoulders, and answered: "Maleesh." (It doesn't matter.) Her voice was low and seductive, but her manner was apathetic. Yes, it was true that she entertained only Mahmoud's most important clients. They came always late at night and left before dawn. It was obvious that she was completely indifferent to all of them.

The longer I talked to the beautiful girl, the more I felt that I was talking to a zombie who at seventeen had forgotten the meaning of the word love.

Then I mentioned the Egyptian, and Maria became like a raging tigress. Her red lips parted in a snarl over her white teeth, and I saw her dig her long nails deeply into the cushions of the divan.

"One day I will kill him," she blazed. "One day I will drive a knife into his heart!"

"If you could do that, Maria, you would rid the world of a devil!" I said rashly. But even before I had had time to regret the remark, she stared at me blankly, so that I knew she did not understand.

But, later, when I left Maria and Mahmoud's brothel I made a silent vow to the stars that the Egyptian would be made to pay for what he had done.

Chapter V

I WAS READY to leave for Asmara when the Egyptian returned from El Obeid. Since he was in his most affable mood, I guessed that his trip had been successful. But when I asked him about it, he answered me evasively and said that since the "affair of Suez" business was bad everywhere. Then he led me on to the veranda.

"We can order drinks out here," he said. "I do not wish George or any of the others to listen to our conversation."

Glancing over his shoulder, he drew four envelopes from his pocket. "These are for you. Please put them away at once."

I watched him relax visibly as I slipped them into my pocket.

"How soon will you be leaving for Asmara?" he asked, wiping his forehead with a scented handkerchief.

"This afternoon. I'm all ready and packed," I told him, and was surprised when he got up and held out his hand.

"In that case, I will not keep you, Mr. John. I wish you *bon voyage*," he said, and then walked back into the hotel.

Up in my room, I took the four envelopes from my pocket and studied the addresses. One was to Big Mama in Asmara, one to an Ethiopian at an address in Addis Ababa, the third to a Greek in Djibouti, and the fourth to an Indian in Crater, at Aden. This last one puzzled me, for while I knew that slavery existed in Ethiopia and French Somaliland, I had never heard of it in Aden.

Despite the fact that Ethiopia, like the Sudan, is a member of the United Nations, all attempts by the Emperor and his Government to stamp out slavery have failed for two reasons. Firstly, because Haile Selassie won his throne by the sword with the support of the rich slave-owning landlords, who to this day have

remained completely feudal. Any attempt to change their way of
life either by the Emperor or the Government would be met by
fierce resistance. Thus, Haile Selassie's decrees regarding the
abolition of slavery have never been enforced, especially in the
south and west where life is as primitive as it was more than a
hundred years ago. Indeed, in many areas Government officials
still dare not show their faces without a strong police escort.

The second reason may be summed up in the single word
"Gaber." This is the name for a system of slavery in Ethiopia
whereby the slaves and their families are allowed to live on the
land and are even given a small portion for their own use. They
are obliged to work on their master's property, but are allowed
to cultivate their own land during whatever free time they can
get.

It has often been argued by the Ethiopian authorities that this is
a form of serfdom and that the landlord is a patriarchal figure
with the welfare of his serfs at heart. But this is manifestly untrue
since the slaves or serfs have no security and can be sold at their
master's whim. In addition to the fact that any member of the
family can be sold separately, the landlords often give away
slaves to discharge a debt. Moreover, if slaves attempt to run
away they are flogged within an inch of their lives. If they
attempt to escape a second time and are caught, their hands are
chopped off as a warning to others. Such punishment virtually
condemns them to a lingering death, since their relatives have
scarcely enough food to keep themselves alive, let alone a man or
woman without hands. If, however, the escaped slaves can reach
Addis Ababa they are technically free. All they need to do is to
go to the nearest policeman and claim the protection of the
Emperor. But to this day, many slaves who fail to reach the
capital join the Shufti or bandits, who infest the Ethiopian high-
lands. In 1957 these bandits had become so numerous and daring
that the Government had to mount two full-scale military
operations against them.

These and many other facts I recalled as I journeyed to Asmara
to deliver the first of the Egyptian's letters.

While in Asmara I discovered that Big Mama was not the king-pin there, although she liked to give the impression that she alone ruled in Eritrea, and that no slaves could be bought or sold without her permission. The fact came about in a curious way. One evening George, her son, and I, were drinking together at Big Mama's place. George, who was getting drunk, began to cast amorous glances at Big Mama's latest acquisition, a superb little fourteen year old half-caste, part Italian, part Ethiopian, and almost white in colour. Big Mama, who always liked business to be business, rebuked him sharply. George flew into a rage, and slamming down his glass turned to me saying, "Let's get out of this whore-house."

We wandered from brothel to brothel, enjoying a drink and a joke with the occupants. Finally, we came to Madame Jan Phillipe's place, the only European brothel in Asmara. Madame Jan, who was Italian, kept three pure Italian girls. They were orphans, whose parents were killed by the Ethiopians at the "liberation" of Eritrea. Madame Jan, a handsome dark-haired woman in her early forties, was reputed to be no mean operator herself, if George could be believed.

We pushed aside the bead curtains and walked towards the small bar. I ordered a drink, in English. At that the only other occupant of the bar, a scowling dark-haired brute of about forty, turned towards us and snarled, "You bloody Britisher." I thought I had not heard aright. I said "Pardon me, sir, what did you say?"

"Pawdon me sir, what did you say," he mimicked. "I said you were an f—ing Britisher." The accent was thick, and I mistook him for a German. "I don't particularly like the Nazis either," I retorted.

"I'm no f—ing Nazi," he shouted, jumping down from his stool. "I fought with you bastards during the war in the Royal Netherlands Air Force, and what did you do, you shot me down, you double-crossing sons of bitches." He advanced towards me, huge fists raised. He was a big hulking fellow, and although he had obviously let himself run to seed through drink was still a dangerous-looking customer, especially in a rough-house brawl.

As he neared me I whipped the sword from the sword-stick I always carried, and stuck the needle-sharp point about an inch from his throat.

"I don't care a damn who you are," I said, "if you advance another step this goes through you." He saw I meant business and reached for the glass on the counter. It was an old bar-room brawler's trick. He would pretend to have a drink, and suddenly throw the beer in my face, blinding me. He would then come in, head down, for a stranglehold. I swept the glass from the counter with my sword, inches from his fingers. George, who had been a silent spectator to all this, grabbed my arm and said, "Let's get out of here." I backed to the door, still keeping the brawler covered with the sword-stick. Outside he mopped his brow, suddenly cold sober.

"Jesu, but that was a near thing," he said.

"Why?" I asked, "who is that bastard anyhow?"

"He is not only the biggest slaver in Africa, but the most dangerous man on two legs," George answered.

"What's his name?" I asked.

"Toni De Jong—er, Flying Officer Toni De Jong."

"Flying Officer?" I asked incredulously.

"Yes," George answered "surprising, isn't it? He was absolutely right when he said that he flew with the Royal Air Force in the Western desert. Now he flies slaves."

"But if he is the king-pin you claim him to be, why did the Egyptian give me a letter to your mother? Why did he not give me a letter to him?"

"Because he hates Britishers," George answered. "If he knew that the Egyptian had anything to do with any Britisher, he would immediately cease to work with him, and they do a lot of business, these two."

"But why this hatred?" I asked.

"You heard him say that the British shot him down," George answered. "I know that to be true, but it goes back a lot longer than that, to the days after the war. Come in here and I'll tell you about Toni De Jong."

He led the way into a small bar, and when our drinks were before us, George said:

"Most of what I know about De Jong comes from himself, but I have met one or two others who knew him after the war, before he became a slaver. One of them was the Egyptian. The other is Carl, a German who deals in Berber girls and does a lot of business with Mama."

De Jong was apparently a very good pilot in the Libyan desert. Even the Germans knew of him there. Carl was also a pilot, with the German Luftwaffe, operating in that area. After the war he applied for a job with KLM Airlines. The Dutch would not give it to him because De Jong says that the British refused to give him something he needed, a reference or something of that sort. This started his hatred of the British. After that he went to Cairo and in 1948 was flying a Spitfire for the Egyptian Air Force in the war against Israel. He used to knock around the bars of Cairo a lot, especially Shepheard's Hotel, but was cold-shouldered by the British there, which increased his hate for them. Here he met the Egyptian, who at that time was mainly in the white-slave racket, and was able to put De Jong on to some tasty bits of stuff, fresh from Europe.

After the Israeli war De Jong went to Ethiopia, where he was employed as an instructor to the Ethiopian Air Force. This job didn't last long. Women and gin, De Jong's two favourite vices, were too easy to come by, and in a short time he was sacked. He hung around the bars and hotels, and met the Ethiopian, who is the master mind of slavery in Ethiopia.

The Ethiopian, who felt sorry for him and was a lonely man himself, supplied him with girls free, and often gave him money for drink.

Then the Egyptian came to Addis with Carl, a German Nazi who stayed behind with the Berber tribe in the Western Desert after the fighting had ended there and repaid his hosts by selling their unwanted daughters to the Egyptian, who in turn sold them to the Ethiopian. The Ethiopian either used them in his own brothels there, or shipped them from Massawa to Saudi Arabia.

They met De Jong with the Ethiopian, and naturally De Jong and Carl, both being fighter pilots during the war in the Western Desert, got together and Carl remembered "the flying Dutchman" as De Jong was called. Suddenly Carl had a brainwave. Why not employ De Jong to fly slave girls to Saudi Arabia? He was a good pilot, and professed to be ready for anything. It would be simple to buy an old Douglas DC3, and fly it from Eritrea to Saudi Arabia. There were plenty of abandoned Italian airfields in Eritrea, the one at Bashar Assoli would do excellently. The Ethiopian and the Egyptian heartily agreed. De Jong, however, was cautious. He turned to the German.

"You were also a good pilot, why don't you fly them?"

"Because, my good friend I am what your British friends call a war criminal. There is always a danger, slight, but nevertheless there, that I might be forced down. If your British friends caught up with me in their territories—" he made an expressive gesture across his throat. Finally, De Jong agreed. The pay would be high and after all he had little to lose.

An old plane was purchased and next night De Jong and the Ethiopian took off for Bashar Assoli, where Carl assured them everything was ready. No sooner had they touched down than their trucks roared up. One carried fuel for the plane and out of the other two De Jong saw twenty girls of all sizes and nationalities emerge. They had two things in common, they were all young, and they were all beautiful. They were chained together by a thin chain which ran from one wrist to the other. De Jong licked his lips. What wouldn't he give for one of those. The Ethiopian, noticing his looks, nodded. "They are beautiful, but not for you, my friend, they fetch eight hundred pounds each in the Saudi market." Then the Ethiopian introduced him to the real owner, a Saudi Arabian and evidently a very important man, judging by the Ethiopian's tone when he spoke to him.

They climbed aboard and the Ethiopian gave De Jong last-minute instruction. "You will fly to Mecca but do not land there, land on a flat strip you will see about five miles outside the city. Disembark the slaves and the Sayed, and return here." De Jong did as he was instructed and returned to Bashar Assoli. He left the plane there and came to Asmara. "That is where I first met him, at Mama's."

"But flying slaves didn't make him the big shot," I said.

"Ah, that comes later," George answered.

"De Jong made many runs without incident, always with the Saudi Arabian. He had money to throw around and was a big spender here in Asmara. Then one day the incident which the German predicted might happen did happen. In 1951 De Jong was spotted by two R.A.F. jet fighters almost over the Kamaran Island just off the Yemen coast. They signalled him to land on the island. De Jong pretended to comply, but as they came lower and lower De Jong suddenly pushed the throttles full forward and swept over the runway to the safety of the Yemen coastline. The jets realised they had been tricked and flew after him. They probably suspected him of delivering arms to the Yemenites. They opened fire. He managed to belly-land just inside the Yemen border. Pulling open the door he dragged the terrified girls from the blazing plane. Looking back he saw that the Saudi was trapped. For some reason he couldn't open his seat-belt. The plane blew up. De Jong looked at the blazing wreck which was the Saudi's funeral pyre. For the loss of a plane, which was not his in the first place, he had become the owner of twenty beautiful young slave girls. They set out to trudge across the desert. Finally, De Jong and nineteen of them, the twentieth had died on the way of heat exhaustion, reached Hodeida in the Yemen.

De Jong had become an apt pupil of the Saudi's and of the Ethiopian's. He approached the official who approximated to the police chief, explained about the the crash and said that the Saudi's last wish was that he, De Jong, should be received hospitably and that the slaves should be sold and the money given to him. He knew that no Arab, no matter how low or greedy, would disrespect the death wish of another. The cowering slaves were sold by public auction and Toni De Jong was the richer by several thousands of pounds.

The Yemenites saw him on his way and a couple of weeks

later he turned up at Big Mama's in Asmara, where he went on a monumental drunk for a week. He then announced to all and sundry that he was no longer a pilot of slaves, he was now in the business as a dealer."

"How did the others take it?" I asked.

George laughed. "De Jong and the Ethiopian had a stand-up fight in Big Mama's," he said. "The Ethiopian accused De Jong of being a thief. He claimed that as he had sold the girls to the Saudi, and as the Saudi was now dead, the girls, or the money obtained for them, should revert to him. Hot words followed and De Jong knocked the Ethiopian out. The Ethiopian never spoke to or dealt with him again."

Here I must say that the Ethiopian never as much as mentioned the name of De Jong to me.

"The Ethiopian and Carl, the German, didn't give a damn. It was a convenient and easy way of getting rid of their slaves. As for Mama, she was only too delighted. He was a good customer in the bar, and often used her girls to avoid spoiling the market value of his own. The Saudis and the Yemenites will pay two hundred pounds more if the girl is a virgin. Then De Jong and Mama fell out. It happened over Maria. De Jong wanted to buy her, and Mama refused, although he offered more than the Egyptian who afterwards bought her. The reason Big Mama wouldn't sell Maria was because De Jong was a sadist, he always flogged his girls before having intercourse with them."

"De Jong bought another plane, and really set up in business. He bought all the girls he could lay his hands on. Ethiopian, Sudanese, Berbers, Egyptians, even two French girls from Algiers, anybody as long as she was young, beautiful, and if possible a virgin. He is absolutely ruthless. I believe he would sell his own sister if he got her out here. Finally, the traffic got too much for Eritrea although De Jong was paying a fortune in bribes. Besides, the old plane was falling to pieces from the constant flying, and servicing it was not easy. He crash-landed it a couple of times and once nearly lost his life. He moved from here to Abd-El-Kuri, an island in the Gulf of Aden, and now delivers by fast motor boats. It is said that he keeps the very best looking girls there, and is starting a baby farm like the Greek has in Djibouti. He must be a millionaire several times over."

When I heard the whole sickening story I felt sorry that I hadn't run the sword through his throat. Fate, however, finally caught up with Toni De Jong. While in Libya last year I went out to Garian. I had an appointment there with Carl von Berg, the German Nazi. It was made through a source that shall remain nameless. There was no mistaking him, a big blond man with duelling scars criss-crossing his face. After some conversation I mentioned my fight with De Jong in Asmara. "Ah, yes, De Jong," the German said, "well he will fight no more." "Why?" I asked.

"Did you not hear? He was cut to pieces during the Iraq rebellion last year."

"What happened?" I asked.

"Well," Carl answered, "you have probably heard that De Jong would buy a woman from anywhere, provided she was young and pretty. This time he went too far. He bought the fourteen-year-old daughter of an important Iraqui Bedouin sheikh, who had been stolen from her home, and sold her in Taizz, in the Yemen. The Iraqui swore vengeance, and the Iraquis have long memories. De Jong had the misfortune to be in Baghdad during the Revolution. They found his body in the Tigris, and could only identify him by his passport. He had been cut to pieces."

"ADDIS ABABA—the name means New Flower—is situated 7,740 feet above sea level and is the capital and commercial centre of Ethiopia. It is beautifully situated in the midst of mountain peaks which tower majestically over its own high elevation and, since it extends over several eucalyptus-covered hills, there is a variation of over 1,000 feet in altitude. It is a city of imposing buildings and wide streets. . . ."

So say the guide-books. But they fail to add that behind the imposing buildings there exist some of the worst hovels in Africa, or that leading from the wide streets are narrow lanes in which are situated innumerable *tedgbas* where a woman or a girl is more easily obtained than a pint of beer in an English pub. Neither do the guide-books tell you that a few miles from the centre of the capital it is possible to buy a male or female slave for far less than the price of a suit of clothes from the local tailor.

Addis Ababa is, in fact, a city where graft and vice are rampant and where the badly needed machinery bought with Point Four funds are by some metamorphosis known only to Africa changed into Cadillacs and other luxuries for government officials.

There are no touts or pimps in Ethiopia since there is no need for them in a country where vice has its own well-defined territory.

The Egyptian had given me a letter for one, Hapte, and told me to ask for him in the bar of the King George Hotel in the centre of the city. It was, the Egyptian said, under new management since I had visited it the previous year. Its former owner, a Greek, was in prison doing a three-year sentence for failing to fly the Ethiopian flag during the numerous national holidays. He had been tried and convicted for "insulting the person of the Emperor, Haile Selassie."

The new manager was an Ethiopian, and judging by the number of flags flying over the hotel, he was taking no chances. The Greeks who had frequented the bar had vanished, and the new customers, who were all Amharas, stared at me with hostility as I came in. A white man is not popular in Ethiopia, despite the millions of dollars the Americans are pouring into the country, for this dislike is a legacy from the days of the Italian invasion.

I asked for Hapte. The manager, who spoke some English, looked at me suspiciously. "There are many Haptes in our country," he said. "Hapte is a first name, like John in your country."

"I'm perfectly aware of that," I told him. "I have been to Ethiopia before. However, the Hapte I'm looking for is a friend of the Egyptian."

He gave a start. "That Hapte. What do you want with him?"

"That is my business," I said firmly. "But if you know him, tell him I have a message for him from the Egyptian."

"We shall see," he answered slyly. "Come back at this time tomorrow night. Perhaps something can be arranged."

That evening when I was returning to my hotel a curious thing happened. I was being driven in a taxi by a driver whom I had known the previous year. He had been a sergeant-major with the Ethiopian forces in Korea and spoke reasonably good English.

As we neared the hotel, two policemen with levelled rifles stepped into the road. Signalling us to stop, they ordered us out of the taxi and told us to put our hands up. Then, they told the driver to tell me that I was to be searched. When he translated this to me, I said that I would refuse to be searched unless they produced an officer who spoke English. When this had been translated to them, one of them grumblingly went off while the other kept me covered with his rifle.

After about five minutes, an English-speaking officer appeared. "What is the meaning of this outrage?" I demanded.

"We are going to search you," he said, "and if you resist we will arrest you."

One of the policemen then went through my pockets, passing my wallet and papers to the officer who studied them carefully. Having read them, he handed them back to me, motioning me to lower my hands.

"What the devil's the meaning of this?" I shouted.

He countered my question with another. "Did you visit the King George Hotel bar tonight?"

"Yes," I told him, "but I didn't know it was illegal to have a drink in Addis."

"Did you ask for a man named Hapte?" he asked, watching me closely.

I decided that the best thing to do was to answer him truthfully, since he was obviously acting on information.

"Yes," I said, "a friend of mine asked me to meet him."

"An Egyptian friend, perhaps?"

"Yes, an Egyptian friend."

"And did he ask you to give this Hapte a message?"

"Yes, he told me to tell him that he was sorry he couldn't come to Ethiopia this year."

The officer laughed. "He was a wise man! Did he give you any other message?"

I shook my head, and he seemed satisfied. "Now, may I go back to my hotel?"

He waved us back into the taxi with reluctance.

As I entered the hotel, the manager, who was a Swiss, came up to me. "The police were here an hour ago, Mr. John. They insisted on searching your room, and there was nothing I could do to prevent them," he apologised, spreading his hands.

I told him not to worry, for I knew that the police in Ethiopia needed no warrant. I knew too that they can arrest without a warrant and hold a person without trial for as long as they wish.

However, I was pretty certain that they had found nothing incriminating in my room. Knowing something of their methods from my previous visit, I had been careful to hide the Egyptian's letters in a waterproof bag in the cistern of my bathroom lavatory. Nevertheless, to their credit, I must admit that although they had been through my room with the proverbial fine toothcomb, not a thing had been disturbed.

My problem now was how to contact Hapte. However, this proved easier than I could have hoped, for he made the contact himself. The day after the police search, the hotel porter came to my room and told me that somebody at the reception desk was asking for the "foreigner with the *yari* (beard)." As I was the only "yarid" man in the hotel, the porter presumed that the stranger was looking for me.

In the foyer a small Ethiopian greeted me with the single word, "Hallo." Then, he led the way outside.

As I followed him, I had the vague feeling that I had seen him the evening before in the bar of the King George.

He bowed me into his waiting car, and said: "Hapte sent me for you."

It could have been a trap. But I decided to take a chance and ran back up the stairs to my room to collect the letter from the Egyptian, taking care to leave the remaining letters in their hiding-place.

Although I knew the city reasonably well, it was some time before I realised that we were driving round in circles. But as we drove up Churchill Road towards the Ras for the third time, I burst out laughing.

The driver looked at me and grinned. "You know Addis Ababa?" he asked.

I told him that I had been there before. "I am driving like this to throw any police off our scent," he explained. "We will circle once more and then go to Hapte's place."

True to his word, he drove once more round the city and then headed out in the direction of the Imperial Palace. But before we reached it, he turned off the main highway to travel down a rough track for about a mile. Finally, we came to a large two-storeyed house standing amongst tall trees. It was surrounded by a

galvanised iron fence topped by vicious-looking spikes. A strong
iron gate blocked our entrance.

The driver sounded his horn twice, and the gate swung open.
We came to a halt before the front door where a tall, handsome
Amhara stood waiting to greet me.

So this was Hapte.

As he led me through the hall of his house into the long cool
living-room giving on to a veranda, he towered over me, and
I could see the powerful muscles of his broad shoulders rippling
under the silk shirt he was wearing.

"This is from the Egyptian," I said, as he waved me into a
chair.

He tore open the envelope, and a silence fell between us as he
read the letter. Then he laughed, showing his strong white teeth.

"That would have been a nice little nest-egg for the police
if they had found it on you last night."

"What do you mean? Nest-egg?" I queried.

Hapte settled himself more comfortably into his chaise longue.

"It's like this, Mr. John," he explained. "For a long time the
police have been trying to establish a connection between me
and the Egyptian. They know that I'm in the business. They
know I own the best brothels in Addis. They know too that I
own slaves, and that I buy and sell slaves. Although Ethiopia
pays lip-service to the United Nations, and although a decree
has been passed in this country forbidding the keeping of slaves,
nobody takes any notice of such details," he shrugged. "Why,
some of the Emperor's staunchest supporters are large slave
owners. Without slaves they could not work their land. But the
exporting of slaves, mainly girls for the harems in the Yemen and
Saudi Arabia, or the brothels in Khartoum, Djibouti and Aden,
is an entirely different matter. That is a criminal offence. Oh,
don't worry, neither you nor I will be sent to prison," he laughed
as I started from my chair. "The police would have arrested you,
and sent me a polite note asking me to come to the station to
discuss matters. When I arrived, they would have produced the
letter you have just delivered, and asked for seven thousand

dollars—roughly one thousand pounds—for the letter and for you. Naturally, I should have paid it," he explained casually. "Otherwise, all business between the Egyptian and myself would have ceased, and our business is worth considerably more than seven thousand dollars."

"What would have happened to me?" I asked.

"You would have been released, and that would have been the end of the matter. As it is, the Egyptian has asked me to pay you seven hundred dollars. In addition, I shall give a further three hundred dollars to the police captain who searched you to ensure that you have no more trouble while you're in Addis Ababa."

That day when I got back to my hotel I tore up the two remaining letters the Egyptian had given me and flushed them down the lavatory. I was taking no more chances.

Chapter VII

DURING THE NEXT few weeks I saw quite a lot of Hapte. He was a remarkable man. Intelligent, widely travelled and utterly ruthless, he had built up his "export business" as he called it, with an astuteness that staggered me. Now, he left it almost entirely to the Egyptian, seldom travelling outside Ethiopia and content to live either in Addis Ababa or in his house at Harar.

Knowing that I could not denounce him, he talked to me quite freely, and I had the feeling that he was glad to do so, for I suspected that he was a lonely man. I knew that he was ostracised by the Ethiopians because of his activities during the Italian occupation, and by the Europeans and the Americans because he owned brothels and was a slave-trader. "Nevertheless, they're glad enough to patronise my brothels," he told me with a bitter laugh.

He admitted that his income was in the region of twenty thousand pounds a year, and I did not doubt that it was true. For he owned seven brothels in Addis: three in the select quarter near the University College, and four along Churchill Road, a notorious brothel district which runs from the main square to the Ethiopian State Theatre. In addition to these, he told me he had an interest in several *tedgbas*, small brothel-cum-beer shops, where the girls were employed on a part-time basis. These were of the lowest class, and the part-time prostitutes were the throw-outs of the other brothels, women who had grown too old or had contracted venereal diseases, and for whom he could not find a buyer outside Ethiopia.

Hapte told me that he was born in Harar, of mixed Arab-Ethiopian stock.

"It was in Harar that I invested my savings in three young girls," he explained. "I brought them to Addis and set up in business in a deserted, tumbledown house near the railway station. That was in the days of the Italian invasion, when Mussolini had sent some whores from Italy to take care of his soldiers. But the demand far exceeded the supply," he grinned.

"At first, few Italians came to my place. But soon the word spread through the garrison that Hapte's girls were between twelve and fourteen years old, and the demand for their services was so great that I had to limit each soldier to fifteen minutes of fun! With the profits I made, I returned to Harar and bought another three girls. And so my business grew and grew, and by the time the war started, I had made my first thirty thousand pounds."

When the Allies invaded Ethiopia, Hapte realised that his dream of an Ethiopian brothel empire was ended, at least temporarily.

"The man who supplied the Italians with native girls was an outcast with the new Government," he said with a sigh. "But I managed to slip across the border into French Somaliland, where I had some contacts from the good old days as I used to buy girls there. After that, I made my way to Djibouti, disguised as a Somali. There, I threw in my lot with a Greek and was able to make a comfortable living supplying girls to the Allied troops. Then what do you think I did?" Hapte asked with a chuckle...

"I've no idea!" I told him.

"I joined forces with that old devil Big Mama!" he roared, slapping his huge thigh. "But times were tough. All but five of my girls had had their throats slit when the Ethiopians decided to kill all those who had collaborated with the Italians. But those five made their way to Asmara to join me.

"It cost me ten thousand pounds to get back into this country. I paid out bribes here and gave presents there, so that when Eritrea was federated with Ethiopia I was free to slip quietly back to Addis. I started again almost from scratch with just a couple of girls. But times had changed, and although the business slowly recovered, it didn't take me long to realise that the big money lay in buying and selling slaves. You see," he explained, "labour was short here as everywhere. I managed to get the names of the land-owners who needed workers. Then, I bought slaves cheaply, for the people were poor, and moved them by night to their new homes, selling them at a handsome profit. The Amhara land-owners were only too pleased to deal with me."

It was but a short step from selling slaves within the country to selling them in the outside market. At first, Hapte himself did the actual selling.

"I travelled thousands of miles through the Sudan, Saudi Arabia, the Yemen, Trucial Oman and Oman," he told me. "Everywhere I found a ready market. In fact, the demand soon exceeded the supply, and I was forced to call on Big Mama for help. The old witch acted as a procurer for me. And I don't mind telling you, we both did pretty well. At that time in Eritrea there were hundreds of children—kids whose ages ranged from ten to fourteen—who were born during the Allied occupation. Most of them had American and British fathers and Ethiopian mothers. The Arab sheikhs, particularly in Saudi Arabia, were willing to pay up to eight hundred pounds for a virgin girl child and as much as five hundred pounds for a pretty boy.

"There were also many Italian-Ethiopian half-castes, and some pure Italian orphan girls for whom the sheikhs would pay as much as a thousand pounds for a virgin. These girls were in great demand in the cabarets and night-spots in Cairo, but the risk of smuggling them into Egypt was terrific. But the profits made it worth taking!" Hapte added, licking his lips.

It was in Cairo that he had first met the Egyptian, who at that time was engaged solely in the white-slave racket. He got girls from France and Italy to travel to the Middle East on the pretext of finding them engagements in the cabarets. Once arrived, he sold them to the brothel keepers.

Hapte and the Egyptian soon went into partnership.

"The arrangement suited me perfectly," Hapte said. "I supplied the slaves and the Egyptian sold them. You see, I was getting fed up with travelling all over the Middle East. What's more, there were some countries where the police were beginning to be suspicious of me. And although I was making a hell of a lot of money, I was giving too much of it away in bribes and presents. In addition, the Ethiopian police had started taking an interest in my affairs, especially in my trips abroad. They didn't mind me dealing in slaves within the country, provided they got their cut. But the Government could hardly keep up its façade in U.N.O. of being a non-slave-owning country if Ethiopian girls and boys were being sold as slaves abroad. But what really decided me to go into partnership with the Egyptian was that the profits from my brothels were falling off. The madames were pocketing too much for themselves."

I asked Hapte one day about the slave caravans through the Sudan to the port of Suakin. "Do many of the slaves come from Ethiopia?"

"Some," he admitted, "although not as many as is generally supposed. It's too expensive and wasteful a method to pay dividends nowadays. For instance, I remember sending a caravan across the border near Akobo—three boys and seven girls, bound for Saudi Arabia through the port of Suakin. They were mainly Gallas, and cost me all of seven hundred pounds. I had paid another thousand pounds to the Arab in charge of the camel train that transported them. On the way, they had to make a wide detour to avoid a detachment of the Sudanese Army who were on manoeuvres in Southern Kordofan. This took time. Worse still, precious food was used up so that the kids had to be strictly rationed. On that trip three of the slaves, two girls and a boy, died. The others arrived looking like skeletons. At the port of Lith I was offered seven hundred pounds for the seven that remained. I had them taken to Mecca where they were fattened up in the house of my agent. Finally, we sold them for two thousand pounds. But what with my expenses, commission to my agent, and the cost of feeding them in Mecca, I was out of pocket on the deal," Hapte grumbled.

"The majority of caravans now come from the Belgian Congo," he went on. "Either there or from French Equatorial Africa, where they have no other means of transporting slaves. So far as we're concerned, we still have the Red Sea and the dhows. Also, we've introduced more modern methods, using light aircraft operating from the wartime Italian and Allied airstrips. No, Mr. John, the slave camel caravans are a bit out of date," he laughed.

Hapte's three hundred dollars must have worked like a charm with the police, for I was never again troubled by them. The detective who had tailed me was withdrawn and I was free to travel wherever I liked.

One evening Hapte invited me to visit his most exclusive brothel, situated in the residential outskirts of Addis Ababa. I went there with an American named Jack, who worked for Point Four.

Jack was an amazing character. An alcoholic who managed to put in more work than anyone else in his organisation, he must have had the constitution of an ox. I often drank and played poker with him and two other Americans until seven in the morning. Then, as three of us tumbled bleary-eyed into bed, Jack shaved, had breakfast, and left for his office to put in a full day's work and get through the best part of a bottle of rye before returning to the hotel for dinner at seven o'clock. He told me that as a prisoner in the Korean war he had been tortured by being kept awake for nights on end, and claimed that this training enabled him to survive whole nights of poker and drink without feeling sleepy.

Jack and I were met at the door of the brothel by the Madame, who knew him well, for he was a regular visitor. She invited us into the drawing-room, and I gave a gasp of astonishment. The room was a perfect example of a Victorian drawing-room down to the last antimacassar and the smallest china ornament crowding the mantelpiece. Then, as Madame dispensed tea from a huge silver tray, the girls were ushered in. I had been expecting girls like those I had seen in Mahmoud's or Big Mama's places. Half-naked creatures, displaying their wares to the best advantage. But these girls were entirely different. They came into the room as demurely as girls from a smart Parisian finishing school, their young bodies discreetly covered up by flowing dresses; only their smooth brown arms were bare. Nevertheless, they were nine of the loveliest girls I have ever seen. Six were Amharas, two I judged to be Italo-Amharas, and one was a beautiful dark Galla girl. It was obvious that the Amharas were of high class from the tattooing around their necks and on their foreheads.

Madame called them forward to be introduced, and as we shook hands with them, each girl bobbed us a dainty curtsy. Then, one of them sat down at the piano and played tinkling waltzes while the rest sipped their tea. I wanted to laugh, for the scene was more like a vicarage tea-party than a brothel.

Jack, who never wasted time, soon chose his girl and departed with her upstairs. Nothing so sordid as money was even mentioned. Jack knew the price—fifty dollars—and would leave that sum in an envelope, specially provided for the purpose, on the mantelpiece in the girl's room.

While Jack was away, Madame and I made polite conversation. She was a high-born Ethiopian lady, whose husband, a senior officer in the army, had been killed fighting against the Italians. Prostitution, she explained, was no disgrace in Ethiopia. In fact, unless a girl found a husband, it was the only career open to her. Although today modern thought and ideas are gradually seeping through into Ethiopia, there are still many parents in that country who would be horrified if their daughters suggested becoming typists or nurses, while they would willingly apprentice them to a brothel at the age of thirteen or fourteen. The custom is traditional with both men and women of Amhara that they will never do any work that involves using their hands. That is why there are still so few Amhara doctors, nurses, typists or shopkeepers in Ethiopia. On the other hand, all Government posts, even the most menial, are staffed by Amhara men. But for the girls there is nothing but the brothel.

Hapte had bought seven Amhara girls when they were between thirteen and fourteen; their parents, high class Amharas, obtaining a good price for them. They were not just ordinary slaves, for under the purchase agreement Hapte was forbidden to sell them abroad or to re-sell them in Ethiopia without their parents' consent. They were to be kept in a high-class brothel only and could not be sent for any reason to the *tedgbas*. If a girl happened to catch a disease, she would be sent home, but the purchase price would not be refunded. If, however, when she reached the age of twenty-one she wanted to leave the brothel, she could do so provided her parents returned to Hapte half the price he had paid for her. Such an arrangement suited Hapte, the girl's parents and the girl. Hapte, because in a country where girls mature early he had half the purchase price of a young girl of fourteen as well as the girl's total earnings for seven years; the parents, because they had the use of the money for that period; and the girl, because the half of the purchase price they retained was her dowry. The fact that she had been a prostitute for seven years in no way barred her to marriage. Indeed, it is considered an attraction, and Hapte told me that many girls leaving his brothels to get married, asked him to purchase their daughters, if they have any, when they too reach the age of fourteen.

If, on the other hand, the girl dislikes the life in the brothel when she reaches the age of twenty-one, or if her looks are fading, she may set up as a private prostitute. Her parents then return half the purchase price to Hapte, and with the balance the girl opens a *tedgbas* in the brothel quarter. This is usually a one or two-roomed hut with a kitchen attached. Having acquired a place of her own, the girl then buys a black slave to attend her, bath her, do her washing and cooking. For no Amhara prostitute, however low, will wash and cook for herself.

The girl in her *tedgbas* is not entirely independent, for Hapte still retains an interest in her, collecting ten per cent of her earnings, as well as sending round his strong-arm men to warn off any of the other girls who may try to interfere with her. All this, of course, applies only to high-born Amhara girls. The half-castes and the black girls are slaves, pure and simple, and unless a rich man fancies one sufficiently to pay half her purchase price when she is twenty-one, they are likely to remain slaves for ever. After the age of thirty they become a liability and quickly go down the scale through the low class brothels to the *tedgbas*, until at last they are thrown out into the streets to survive as best they can. A few do survive by begging and stealing. The majority, having no hope left, quickly die.

When Jack returned, we took our leave of Madame. He thought me a fool for not going with one of the girls, for to him the Amhara girls were the world's best lovemakers, and he had plenty of experience. In this brothel, he told me that every girl had two black slaves to attend her. That afternoon when they had gone to the girl's room to undress, two tubs of hot water were brought in. The girl sat in one and Jack in the other. Then, two young negresses washed them thoroughly, afterwards rubbing their bodies with aromatic oil. After the lovemaking this performance was repeated.

In such first-class brothels there was no time limit. For fifty dollars a man might stay an hour or a night. Indeed, they still talk about the American army officer, stationed in Asmara, who spent a nine-day leave in Addis Ababa, spending each night with a different girl in Madame's establishment!

Hapte suggested that I might like to visit a low-class *tedgba*. Few white men, he said, had ever seen one, except the occasional drunken American or a Greek or an Italian who was too poor to afford the better class places. He warned me to go armed as there was always the possibility of being attacked and robbed. He also warned me on no account to have anything to do with the girls, many of whom were diseased, and all of whom were thieves. We could account for our presence in the quarter by pretending to be drunk, as native beer was sold there.

When the night came for our visit, there was no need for Jack to pretend he was drunk. He was drunk.

My taxi man drove us to the *tedgba*, a two-roomed mud-floored shack, stinking to high heaven of sweat and human excrement. There were about twenty natives squatting and lying in various stages of drunkenness in the room measuring eighteen feet by thirty. Amongst them were six or seven women and girls. The eldest was an old hag of forty. The youngest could not have been more than fourteen. All of them were stark naked.

From an inner room came laughter, squeals and sounds of slaps. In one corner of the outer room was a makeshift bar of old packing cases, and on a shelf behind it stood rows and rows of bottles of beer. The bar was presided over by the only fully dressed woman in the room; a hard-faced Amhara of about forty whom I took to be the madame.

As we came in the room fell silent. Jack staggered to the bar, stepping on or over some of the bodies sprawled on the floor. When Madame saw him stagger, she smiled. Here, that smile seemed to say, were some rich pickings.

I slipped the safety catch of the .32 revolver in my pocket. Jack ordered two beers. We drank it out of the bottles, preferring not to use the filthy chipped glasses standing on the counter.

The conversation started up again. From a group of five or six in one corner came angry mutterings. There was only one thing to be done. I called for drinks all round. We were almost trampled underfoot in the rush to the bar. Only three of the crowd that filled that stinking room failed to come up for their drinks. They were flat out; unconscious on the floor.

Madame spoke English of sorts, and she asked us if we wanted any of the girls. The cost, she said, three Ethiopian dollars a time. About nine shillings. We could take our pick. Then, she called them up one by one, but remembering Hapte's advice, we turned them down on one pretext or another. One was too old, another too fat, another too thin, and so on.

Madame's face fell, as she interrupted the lovemaking in the other room to bring us two more girls who were in there. They were both about twelve or thirteen and as naked as the day they were born. We refused them on the grounds that they were too old! Then Madame became exasperated. There was no chance of stealing our wallets unless she could lure us into the inner room, and this she was obviously determined to do. She whispered something into the ear of one of the women, who immediately slipped on her dress and went out. In a few minutes she returned with two fuzzy-haired imps. They couldn't have been more than ten years old.

"Are they young enough?" Madame asked anxiously.

It was time to get out. We bowled over two Amharas in our dash for the door. I had kept the taxi waiting, and as we jumped into it I could still hear Madame cursing us at the top of her lungs.

IT WAS A few days after our visit to the *tedgba* that Hapte told me he was going to Harar to buy some girls and asked me to go with him.

I had finished my work in Addis Ababa, and since Harar was *en route*, I could fly to Dire Dawa, and from there travel by road to Harar. When I returned to Dire Dawa I could get an Ethiopian Airways plane direct to Djibouti.

Dire Dawa—the Empty Plain—is a town set in the middle of nowhere. Its only claim to recognition is that in it are the repair yards of the Franco-Ethiopian railways, employing about four thousand workers. Until the coming of the railway it was a village of mud huts. Now it boasts a hotel of sorts, a church and a number of stone houses.

Harar, on the other hand, was a city long before Addis Ababa was built. It lies thirty-four miles to the south-east of Dire Dawa and has a population of 34,000, predominantly Arab. It was captured in the sixteenth century by the Arabs, who built the magnificent mosque there. They also built, with slave labour, a wall twenty feet high, right round the city. This wall still stands, but the city has overspilled into the neighbouring countryside. Inside the wall are narrow streets and houses built round courtyards with the iron-studded doors of an Arab city. The town has always been the centre of slavery, and although the slave market no longer exists, slaves can still be bought freely there.

The town is situated high in the mountains, the road from Dire Dawa climbing through wild, almost savage, country. It is a narrow road of hairpin bends, where the slightest miscalculation could send a car hurtling down a sheer drop of thousands of feet into the ravine below. To add to the hazards, it is the country of the Danakil, that wild mountain tribe who have never been subdued by either the Arabs, the Amharas or the Italians.

During the occupation, the Danakil were hunted like vermin and thousands of lire were offered for the heads of any Danakil, man, woman or child. The men, to prove their virility, castrate any man they capture, and no Danakil may present himself to his future father-in-law to ask for the hand of his daughter unless he has a pair of testicles hanging on a cord round his neck. The more testicles he has, the greater his virility, and the less dowry he has to pay. Even today the police in Dire Dawa insist on a traveller having an escort when he goes to Harar.

Two years ago an American who travelled from Harar to Dire Dawa was ambushed. He was dragged from his car and his testicles cut off. The car was looted and set on fire, and then pushed over the edge of the road into the ravine. The American was left bleeding by the roadside. Five hours later, he was found dead by a convoy travelling from Harar.

An expedition was sent in pursuit of the Danakils, who retreated further and further into their mountain fortress. Finally, the expedition had to admit defeat and return to Harar empty-handed.

For obvious reasons Hapte did not ask for a police escort for his journey to Harar, but we took the precaution of travelling fully armed. In addition to our revolvers, Hapte had secured a rifle.

We left Dire Dawa at midday. The sun blazed down, and soon my shirt and shorts were soaked in sweat. But as we climbed into the mountains it gradually became cooler, until about halfway up I was forced to borrow the driver's overcoat.

We saw some Danakils on the hills, but they left us alone. Early morning or at dusk are their favourite times for staging an ambush, and most people who are new to the country leave Dire Dawa when it is cool. But Hapte, an old hand, chose to travel at midday.

There is a good hotel in Harar, built during the days of the Italian occupation, and there I stayed, while Hapte lodged with friends.

The following morning, he invited me along to see the girls he was buying. The sale, if one can call it such, was conducted in the courtyard of the house owned by his agent, an Arab. Normally, Hapte would have relied on this agent's judgment in buying the girls, but this seemed to be a special occasion, and I suspected, although Hapte never told me the contents of the letter I had delivered, that these girls were destined for shipment abroad, to fulfil part of the Egyptian's order.

Hapte had already explained to me that in these parts either the landlords or the parents brought the girls to be sold, and raids seldom took place. Elsewhere in Ethiopia, however, particularly along the Sudan and Belgian Congo borders, his agents often organised raids, mainly into those countries. Such raids were mainly for slaves who would be sold for domestic work or work on the land, and only rarely was a girl captured who would be suitable to work in a brothel.

However, the girls being paraded today were the best looking in the area, having been specially selected.

Hapte's agent was an imposing looking man of about fifty, who I knew had been supplying his employer with girls since he had first started business in Addis Ababa during the Italian invasion.

He told us he had scoured the countryside for these girls, and having selected a dozen, told their parents or the man who owned them to bring them to the house so that Hapte could pick the most suitable.

When we had finished our coffee, a servant told the agent that all was ready, and then unlocked the door leading into the courtyard. There was a babel of voices and a rush, as parents, owners and girls shouted at the tops of their voices, apparently extolling the virtues and beauties of their charges.

All the girls were between the ages of twelve and fifteen, and, as usual, all were stark naked. Nor did any of them try to hide their charms. Some had red circles painted round their breasts, the nipples being daubed with a white substance, either chalk or clay. There were two Indian girls amongst them, one with long black hair reaching almost to her buttocks was a real beauty. They came from Dire Dawa, where there is a large Indian community, the majority of whom live in squalor in one special quarter near the railway yards.

Indians are exceedingly fond of children, and I wondered what force of economic circumstances had driven the parents of these youngsters to offer them as slaves. I noticed that their parents were the only people in the courtyard who did not crowd forward around our table. Instead, they stood slightly apart from the rest, the mother of the long-haired girl weeping miserably.

After much shouting and gesticulating some sort of order was restored. The parents and owners were pushed into one corner of the courtyard, while the girls were lined up against the opposite wall. As the Arab called their names, they came forward one by one.

Hapte examined each one of them carefully, looking at their hair, teeth, hands and feet, pinching the soft flesh of their buttocks, and ordering them to run round the courtyard. With the exception of the two Indian girls, they all seemed anxious to please.

Finally, after a protracted consultation with his agent, he selected six, including the beautiful young Indian.

Chapter IX

DJIBOUTI, IN FRENCH SOMALILAND, is one of the hottest places on earth in summer. With its wide tree-shaded streets, public square surrounded by bistros with their tables straying on to the pavements, and its stinking pissoirs, it is a typical French colonial town. Once it was a thriving port through which the bulk of the imports for Ethiopia and the Southern Sudan passed. The railway to Addis Ababa proved a convenient link with Ethiopia, fully justifying the foresight of the French company which built it.

Today, however, the port is almost deserted. For now ships laden with cargoes for Ethiopia are diverted to the new port of Massawa. The railway managed to keep going for a time by raising its freight rates until they reached a point when it was no longer economical for importers to use it.

There is, nevertheless, one trade which still flourishes and has since the war been able to watch its import and export figures steadily rising. The slave trade. Many slaves from the southern parts of Ethiopia are taken overland to Djibouti from where they are shipped across the Red Sea to the nearest point on the Yemen coast. There they are met by the slavers from Taiz, where there is a large market for slaves. Some are bought for work in the Yemen, while others are re-exported to Saudi Arabia. A few Somalis are also exported in the same way. The French authorities do their best to stop this loathsome traffic. But in the slave trade money talks, and there will always be corrupt officials everywhere.

The Greek, to whom I was supposed to deliver the Egyptian's letter, owned an hotel in the main square of Djibouti. I had stayed there on a previous visit, and he had suggested I visit a certain house in the red-light quarter if I needed entertainment. I did not go, but some officers from a Swedish tanker with whom I had been drinking had taken the Greek's advice. The following morning they had told me that the "entertainment" far outdid anything they had seen in Port Said, Tangiers or Marseilles.

The Greek was a huge, hairy man, and gossip had it that he had run one of the most successful "listening posts" for the Germans in that area during the war. It was said that many an Allied ship proceeding along the Red Sea route had gone to the bottom because of him. At the end of the war he was duly tried by a joint Anglo-French military court. The French wanted to shoot him, but the British had insisted that there was not sufficient evidence, and he was released.

He returned to his old profession of supplying girls to the local troops.

When I told him that I had destroyed the Egyptian's letter, he cursed me for a solid five minutes in as many different languages.

"That letter was important," he screamed. "For six months I have been without news of the Egyptian. How can I do business in this way? If he wishes to deal with me he had better come to see me himself. Tell him so from me!"

"It's nothing to do with me," I told him. "He gave me a letter to deliver to you. After something that happened in Ethiopia, I considered it too damned dangerous to carry around any of his letters. So I destroyed them. It was just as simple as that'"

I thought he was going to set about me, as he clenched his great hirsute fists, so I turned on my heel and walked out of his hotel.

A few days later when I met him in the street, he apologised for his outburst, blaming his behaviour on the fact that he was upset at the loss of business due to the "Suez affair." He was accompanied by a tall Somali whom he introduced as his business manager.

I gathered that since the war the French authorities had watched the Greek pretty closely, and he complained bitterly of the vast sums he had been obliged to part with in bribes. Worse still, since General de Gaulle had assumed power, there were rumours that a new set of officials were being sent to French Somaliland. As the Greek had to act with caution he left most of his business to the Somali, who struck me as an interesting character. He spoke good English, and claimed to have been a sergeant in the British Army, although he seemed somewhat hazy about his regiment.

His present job was recruiting women to fill the brothels, and to collect girls and boys for shipment to the Yemen and Saudi Arabia. He told me that the years since the war had been the best he had ever known. In every country along the Red Sea and the Gulf of Aden the vigilance of the authorities had been relaxed so that it was possible to ship slaves with impunity. In Africa slaves could be bought cheaply, and hunger was a great inducement to parents to sell the unwanted members of their families. The Somali boasted that he had often bought and shipped as many as twenty slaves in a single week.

One evening he took me into the brothel quarter of Djibouti. The women were all slaves in the sense that they had been bought by the Greek, who in turn had sold them to the brothel keepers. I found it impossible to estimate their numbers, but the Somali assured me that there were three hundred in the various houses. The majority of them were Ethiopians and Somalis, but here and there I saw girls who were clearly Arabs and Indians.

There was no class distinction as in Ethiopia. All the girls lived in the same squalid huts grouped around a central building which housed the madame. Again, unlike Ethiopia, each madame employed a number of pimps to tout for customers, and the competition between the various houses was fierce. Almost all the customers were sailors from the merchant ships that docked at Djibouti, or soldiers from the local garrison and sailors from the French fleet on the station. I soon discovered that every taxi driver was a pimp working for his own particular madame.

I asked the Somali if the clients did not sometimes object to the girls offered to them or to the filthy squalor of their surroundings. He seemed surprised. "Why should they?" he asked. "They get what they come for—a girl—and after months at sea any girl looks beautiful to them. Besides, they are usually too drunk to notice what they are getting by the time they reach here. In fact, they are often so drunk that they can't do anything with the girls when they get them on the bed," he laughed. "I remember one ship's bo'sun who came here six times and never once managed to have a girl. We give him a bed and take him back to his ship in the morning. He always comes because he knows we won't rob him. The Greek is very strict about that. Drunken men must never be robbed. You see, if complaints were made to the police, there would be investigations and hell to pay. Last week the Norwegian steward of a tanker was robbed here. Luckily, he talked about it in the Greek's bar instead of at the police station. The Greek called him aside, gave him back the money he said he had lost, and then came down here to ask a few questions. Madame and the girl both swore they hadn't robbed the Norwegian. But the Greek found the money hidden in Madame's bedroom. He gave her and the girl fifty lashes over their bare backsides. It will be a long time before either of those bitches steal again," the Somali added with a grin.

"Aren't you afraid that the women might complain to the police?" I asked.

"Not —— likely!" he laughed. "If they did, they'd know what to expect. They would end up with their throats cut."

In Djibouti I saw the only slave baby farm of my tour. The Somali showed me round, and seemed as proud of it as if all the babies were his own. There were thirty-eight of them, ranging in age from three to thirteen. Ten of them were boys.

"This was the Greek's idea," the Somali told me. "It came to him after the war. The women in the brothels were having half-caste babies of all races. So the Greek reasoned it out and decided that if he kept the best-looking kids, in ten years or so he would have a valuable commodity to sell at high prices overseas. So he set two houses aside in the brothel area, each managed by an ex-whore. Half-caste kids were taken to them after they were born, their mothers being paid two pounds for each kid.

"The kid was kept in one house until it was about three, and for the first six months the mother was allowed to visit it and nurse it. If after three years these brats showed signs of growing up pretty, they were moved to the bigger house for schooling."

"Schooling?" I asked. "What do you mean?"

The Somali laughed. "They were taught the tricks of their trade. To make themselves look pretty and to be obliging. When they were about thirteen, the Greek usually sold them to the Egyptian who passed them on to the slave traders from the Yemen or Saudi Arabia. It was their responsibility to collect the kids and ship them to their own countries.

"A good-looking half-caste girl of twelve fetches as much as three hundred pounds. We get a couple of hundred for the boys and we sell most of them to Arabs who seem to like them better than girls. There's no accounting for taste," the Somali added philosophically.

Prior to the Suez affair, he told me, the Egyptian had always travelled personally to Djibouti to select children.

"What happens to the ugly children?" I asked him.

"Oh, most of them are sold over the Ethiopian border. But we get such a small price for them that it's hardly worth the trouble," he added offhandedly.

One evening I met the Somali, who was very drunk, in the bar of the Hotel Europa. The moment he saw me he rushed up. "Here's a good Englishman," he shouted, "better than the whole shower of you f——," using a good old British Army word. I thought he, or I, or both of us would be slaughtered by the whites present. However much the French may preach equality in the colonies, they certainly do not practise it, and they stand no nonsense from "les noirs." However, the Somali was an exceptional man. He was an alcoholic and occasionally became blind drunk but although he shouted a lot in this state he was harmless and was tolerated. When drunk, though, he never entered the bar owned by his boss, the Greek. The French tolerated him for another very good reason—he knew all their secrets, who visited the brothels, who liked to have girls sent to their houses, who liked little boys and so forth. The Somali arranged everything for them, and about these matters was as close-lipped as a confessor.

The Somali's binge on this occasion was apparently caused by the visit of a man he described as a "black f—— Jew" from Saudi Arabia. He was a Senegalese, come to buy boy and girl slaves from the baby farm. It was the Somali's job to show him round, and apparently on the last occasion he bought slaves in Djibouti "the black bastard" left without giving the Somali "as much as would quench his thirst." Most of the other dealers gave him a large tip for his trouble, in addition to the money they paid the Greek.

The Somali had to show the Senegalese round the baby farm that evening, and as time went on and we drank together I wondered if he would be on his feet when the time for the visit came. He had conceived a liking for me, declaring that I was the best "f—— Englishman he had ever met." When he left to pick up the Senegalese he was tottering.

To my amazement, half an hour later, he appeared outside the hotel in a taxi. He sent the driver in for me, and when I went out he was leaning back mouthing every obscenity he had ever heard in the British Army. The Senegalese, obviously terrified, was sitting huddled in a corner and when the Somali saw me he shouted—"Come in here, Mr. Englishman, and we'll take this fat black pig and dump him into the harbour." I attempted to reason with him; although he was a slaver and a rogue, he was a likeable one, and I didn't want him to get into trouble with the Greek. He finally insisted that I should accompany him to the baby farm with the "blue-arsed baboon" who was sitting beside him. Fortunately for the Senegalese, he didn't understand English, but I think he got the import of the Somali's words all right.

We got into the car and drove to the brothel quarter which is down near the docks. The Somali had acquired a bottle of whisky from somewhere, and insisted that I and the driver share it. The "blue arsed baboon" didn't drink, at least I presume he didn't, the Somali never offered him the bottle, except to spill some on him as the car lurched about. We finally pulled up at a large two-storey house. By this time I was swaying slightly and the Somali was well away. He hammered at the door, which was opened by a Somali woman of about fifty, who I gathered was the mistress of the establishment. She said something in Arabic to the Somali who replied by planting a large kiss on her cheek. She led us inside into a kind of sitting-room, and the Senegalese explained the purpose of our visit. His Arabic was slightly different from the Arabic I knew, certain words were pronounced differently but I was able to gather that he wanted seven girls between the ages of ten and thirteen and five boys of similar ages for an important gentleman in Saudi Arabia. The girls had to be as near white as possible. The Somali woman said she would have all the children of these ages ready as soon as possible. She explained that they were all in bed and asleep at that time. While she was away the Somali and I finished the remainder of the whisky between us and the Senegalese, who was dressed in European clothes, kept glancing at his watch.

After about half an hour the Somali woman returned, and led us up some stairs into a large room with rope beds all along the walls, for all the world like an English school dormitory. In the centre of the room there was a large round leather-coloured pouf, about three feet from the ground. Kneeling on it were twelve little girls, with their heads bent towards the centre, so that they formed a circle. Each wore a short cotton vest, pulled well above her waist, so that her protruding buttocks were bare. This was the inspection dais. The girls were near white or chocolate coloured; two who were about thirteen and ten could easily have been mistaken for Southern French or Italian girls. The Senegalese slowly walked around the circle, pinching a buttock here, pulling the cheeks apart there. I noticed that on several of the buttocks were the red marks of the cane. A cane was hung over every bed, and apparently was each girl's personal, and often used, possession from the age of six until she was sold from the baby farm. "Why does he inspect their buttocks first?" I asked the Somali in a whisper. He shrugged. "All these agents for the Saudis do," he said, "I believe every one of them is a f—— homosexual." When the Senegalese had completed the inspection of the girls' buttocks he came up to the Somali and pointed to nine of them. I noticed that the near white girls were among the nine. The remaining three were taken by Madame to another room, and the nine were ordered to lie face upwards on the dais, first removing their vests. The Senegalese now went around the circle again, this time pulling each girl's legs apart, and examining her vagina carefully, carefully noting that the hymen was unbroken. Then to my surprise he pulled a stethoscope out of his breast pocket, and proceeded to examine each girl's back and chest carefully. If not a doctor he certainly had a knowledge of medicine, as the job was done professionally. He made some notes in a notebook he took from his pocket. Finally when he had finished, he pointed to seven of the girls. The Somali, hardly able to see the paper, wrote seven names on the back of an envelope, and the examination of the girls was over. What surprised me most during all this was that the girls never cried or uttered a whimper during all that had passed.

We were led by the Somali woman to another room, where almost the same procedure was gone through. Ten boys were ranged in a circle on a dais, their buttocks towards us. They were all naked, and I saw with horror that five had been castrated. This time the examination of the buttocks was much more thorough, each boy's anus being inspected carefully. Only the five castrated boys were further inspected. I noticed that the scrotum had been entirely removed. The Somali said later that only about ten per cent of the boys are castrated; they are mainly purchased by Saudi Arabian homosexuals, or Yemenites who own harems, as guards. When the Senegalese examined the boys with the stethoscope he rejected one of them immediately. The boy probably suffered from tuberculosis, which is very prevalent in these parts. When the examination was fully over the boys, whose ages ranged between ten and twelve, were led away, all crying bitterly.

The Somali explained next morning when I met him that the next stage of the proceeding would be the completion of the deal between the Senegalese and the Greek. He would be called in to advise the Greek on the probable market value of the slaves selected; it was then up to the Greek to accept or reject the Senegalese's offer. If the offer was accepted transport would be arranged, usually by fast sailing dhow. I put the question that had kept puzzling me. Why had the girls accepted their fate without a murmur, while the boys howled and cried? "Simple," said the Somali, "we tell the girls from a very early age, seven or eight, that they are made for love, what you would call the facts of life. At the age of nine we let them practise with each other, and a year later with boys, taking care, of course that the hymen will not be broken. We show them how to give men exquisite pleasure. Sometimes I even bring my French friends whom I can trust here, and allow the little girls to practise on them. They believe that they are destined for a life of ease, that the days are a long procession of love making. Poor bitches, we don't tell them what the Saudi harems are really like, jealousy, spite, beatings, Lesbianism, with an occasional night in the master's room which only serves to whet their appetites. Let them keep their dreams as long as they can I say.

"With the boys things are different. They have an easy time here, they have no work to do, and probably have homosexual affairs with each other, as well as the girls we allow to practise on them. They know instinctively that life can never be so good again. So they cry, and howl. Such is life. And now I must go to the baboon. You really should have let me throw him into the harbour last night."

Chapter X

I FLEW FROM Djibouti to Aden and found that this was one of the most difficult countries of all to enter. In Djibouti, I had seen the British Consul, Mr. Ballard, who gave me a visa, assuring me that I was lucky to be only on a short visit to Aden as it was the worst possible time of the year for visiting the colony. With these comforting words I boarded the plane from Djibouti, where the thermometer already registered 110 degrees.

Could any place be hotter? I wondered as I sat dripping with sweat in the plane. The question was soon answered, for as we landed in Aden the heat swept over us as from a blast furnace. But I forgot the heat soon after landing, when I marched into the immigration office, where it was, if anything, hotter than outside.

The Indian, who appeared to be in charge of the office, examined my passport, looked at the visa, and then quietly informed me that I would have to pay a deposit of one hundred and fifty pounds to enter the Colony. I explained that I had arranged in Djibouti for a cheque to be sent from England to a bank in Aden, and that all I had in my pocket was about one hundred and fifty shillings. I also remarked that Mr. Ballard had made no mention of this one hundred and fifty pounds deposit.

"I don't give a damn for Mr. Ballard," he said. "You pay the money or we put you on the next plane back to Djibouti."

It was then that my Irish temper, never far below the surface, took over. In a few well chosen words I told him what I thought of him, his immediate ancestors, and his unmentionable forebears. Then, I ended up by demanding that he produce the senior immigration official in Aden.

Since it was then nine o'clock on a Sunday evening, this was manifestly impossible. But I didn't stop to think, and continued to ask for the senior official, while the Indian, by now thoroughly excited, protested that this could not be arranged. Soon, a crowd gathered which included three or four policemen.

Finally, we compromised. The Indian agreed to telephone the senior official, while I agreed to withdraw all my statements concerning the illegitimacy of his ancestors.

By a lucky chance the senior official was at home, and the Indian put me through to him. But when I explained my predicament he laughed. That was the last straw.

"It's no goddam laughing matter," I shouted into the telephone. "Here I am ready to be deported back to Djibouti, with about five pounds in my pocket, and all you do is laugh!"

"Cool down, man," came his answer. "We'll soon put that right."

I handed the receiver back to the Indian. I do not know what his boss said to him, but whatever it was it proved effective, for I have never been cleared through the immigration and customs so quickly before, nor was the one hundred and fifty pounds deposit mentioned again.

I found the Indian in Crater without difficulty. His establishment, which was almost directly behind the Police Training School, was known to all the taxi drivers. It was patronised by sailors who didn't want or couldn't afford to pay the fare out to Sheikh Othamn, the recognised brothel quarter of Aden. It was, in fact, the only brothel in Aden, since the British Colonial authorities do not like such houses in the centre of their cities, and keep them tucked away in the desert. Thus, Aden has its Sheikh Othman, Nairobi its Eastleigh, Port Sudan had—and still has under Sudanese rule—its redlight quarter, and all are isolated from the centre of the towns.

The Indian, as I had suspected in Khartoum when the Egyptian had given me a letter to him, was merely a front for the slave trader. For although Indians in Africa and the Middle East are involved in all kinds of shady deals, such as drug peddling, gold smuggling and prostitution, I have never heard of one in the slave trade. Although profits are high, the risks are great, and the Indians prefer to take no chances.

When I told the Indian that I had destroyed the letter that had been given to me to deliver to him, he pretended at first not to know what I was talking about. He was, he insisted, a simple man running a brothel as best he could. If I wanted one of his girls, well and good. He kept a nice selection of Indian girls, but slaves he knew nothing about. If somebody had given me a letter for him it could only have been by mistake. I left him and returned to Steamer Point.

A few days later I was walking into the Crescent Hotel where I was staying when one of the innumerable pimps who hang around there accosted me. I thought he was touting for custom, and was about to tell him to go to hell, when he said: "You the gentleman who had letter for my Indian friend?"

"Who are you?" I asked.

"I am friend of man the letter was for," he answered. "He say I bring you to him."

Evidently, the bush telephone had been at work, and the last day or two had been spent checking up on me to make sure that I was not from the police.

I went with the messenger to a bar used mainly by the better class natives. There, my guide introduced me to a Yemenite who was sitting alone in a corner. After ordering our drinks, the guide withdrew. There followed a casual conversation during which I guessed that my companion was taking stock of me.

Satisfied, he asked: "You have a letter for me, Mr. John?"

I shook my head. "I had a letter for an Indian brothel-owner in Crater, but I destroyed it."

"Why did you do that?"

"If you must know, I realised it was too dangerous to carry around. My friend who gave me several such letters in Khartoum appears to be in pretty deep water," I told him.

He looked at me shrewdly. "As you say, in deep waters. Of course, you mean the Egyptian?"

I knew then that he was my man. "Yes," I answered. "But what has all this got to do with you?"

"As my friend who brought you here told you, I am the man for whom the letter was intended. Did you, perhaps, read the letter before destroying it?"

"No," I said. "After what happened, I thought that the less I knew about the whole business the better."

"Perhaps you were right," he said reluctantly, "although it is very inconvenient for me. It means that I shall have to send a man to Khartoum. The Egyptian cannot come here and he does not trust the mail."

"Surely it is perfectly safe to post a letter from Khartoum to Aden," I queried.

The Indian smiled. "Believe me, strange things are happening in Khartoum just now. The Egyptian knows what he is doing."

Then, changing the subject, he asked me if I had ever been out at Sheikh Othman. I told him that I had been there two years ago, but at the time I had been too drunk to remember much about it.

"Then, perhaps, you will be my guest there tonight?" he asked.

Seeing the look of doubt on my face, he hastened to add: "Oh, you don't have to have a woman unless you wish. We are not that short of business. In fact, at the moment we have more trade than we can cope with."

That night we drove out to the Sheikh Othman. It is a native quarter some ten miles from Aden. Whole streets are given over to prostitution, and the girls in the brothels are of all shapes, sizes and colours from near white to pitch black.

The Yemenite seemed to be Mr. Sheikh Othman himself, for he was known everywhere we went.

In most of the houses there appeared to be but two or three

girls, and their customers were mostly sailors from the ships in the port, with a sprinkling of servicemen.

I soon discovered that the girls were all slaves, but slaves with a difference. They were well treated, well fed and well clothed. Any girl was free to leave if she did not like the life. A great number were Yemenites, smuggled across the border into the Protectorate and then brought by devious routes to Sheikh Othman. It was a two-way traffic, for any babies, boys or girls, born to the prostitutes were smuggled out into the Yemen as soon as they were old enough to stand the journey.

The Yemenite told me that the girls were encouraged to have children, especially by white men. For if a girl had a near-white baby girl, she was given a bonus of twenty pounds when the child was taken from her. These children fetched high prices in the Yemen, a territory almost closed to whites, and which has little opportunity of acquiring near-white children except through these channels.

On this subject it is worth quoting Claudie Fayen, the French woman doctor, who wrote in her book, *A French Woman Doctor in the Yemen*, published in 1955: "An Ambassador from Saudi Arabia is at the moment the guest of the Del-el-Diaffa," she wrote. "He wishes to buy the young slave of a prince of Sanaa to offer her to his master, the son of King Ibn Saud. A servant from the house of his host comes to warn me secretly of it. He brings me even the contract, already signed. The price agreed is 2,800 thalers or about 700,000 francs (£650). But the conclusion of the bargain is subject to medical examination which will be entrusted to me. The reason the girl costs so much is because she is white."

I must confess that all my information about slavery in the Yemen is second-hand. I had no opportunity of going there and finding out for myself. Moreover, the Yemenite was reticent on the subject, professing to know little about it. Later, I understood the reason for this. When girls were smuggled across the frontier from the Yemen into the Protectorate they did not come empty handed. Each one brought with her a rifle and a bandolier of ammunition hidden amongst her belongings. The Yemenite is one of the leaders of the Free Aden Movement, and also was one of the instigators of the bloody riots that rocked Aden in the autumn of 1958. He did admit, however, that there were many thousands of slaves in the Yemen and that the country was a clearinghouse for slaves brought from the Sudan, Ethiopia and Djibouti who were landed on its coasts. This fact is borne out by another doctor writing in *Le Monde* in August, 1955. He is Doctor Abdelaziz Khaldi and he writes from the Yemen point of view, arguing that it is not a question of slave trading but rather one of a permanent state of slavery which envelops almost all the people.

Perhaps the most revealing account of slavery in the Yemen, particularly with regard to women in the harem, was told to me by a German woman doctor who had been medical officer for a number of years to the Emir's harem, where there were two hundred concubines in the harem.

"My work," she told me, "consisted chiefly in keeping the girls healthy and performing an occasional operation. Slavery as practised in the harem didn't shock me, for I considered that the concubines were far better off than the women outside whose task it is to slave for their menfolk twenty-four hours of the day.

"On the whole, the women in the harem were well treated, had good food, and except for the boredom of their existence, were reasonably happy.

"One job I hated, and that was examining the girls who had been punished for breaking the rules of the harem. They were whipped on their bare behinds by a woman known as the *umm-el-hareem*—the mother or mistress of the harem. This brute used a whip with five thongs, and the blows she administered varied according to the nature of the offence, numbering from five to as many as twenty.

"I was able to save some of the girls from punishment by certifying them as unfit. But that only postponed the evil day.

"Only one offence was severely punished; attempting to escape from the harem. For this a special whip with five knotted lashes was used. The wretched girl was stripped and spread-eagled in the courtyard, where the other inmates of the harem were forced to gather round to watch the punishment. It was administered by a eunuch attached to the harem. A huge, powerful negro, who seemed to enjoy his task thoroughly. Seventy lashes were given, and long before the punishment was over the poor girl fainted. But the negro went on lashing the unconscious girl until the allotted number of strokes had been given. It usually took a girl months to recover from this brutal treatment. Eunuchs, being physically frustrated creatures, take a sadistic delight in inflicting pain on women and are known to be notoriously cruel," she added.

From this German doctor I learned a lot about the eunuchs who serve the harem.

"Contrary to common belief," she told me, "not all eunuchs are incapable, and it is wrong to imagine that castration renders them free from sexual desires. It is a fact that the eunuch who has only lost his testicles can still have an erection and can go on enjoying sexual intercourse. Naturally, this leads to orgies in the harem where the women take advantage of the fact that they can enjoy the eunuch's affections without risk of becoming pregnant. Because of this, the eunuch often has his penis removed as well as his testicles. This ghastly operation is performed mostly before the boy has reached the age of puberty, and for ever afterwards it is only possible for him to urinate through a tube or quill."

This same doctor confirmed the stories I had heard that white or near-white girls were in big demand for the harems of the Yemen.

"A sure way to win the esteem of the Emir Sheikh is to present him with a white or light-skinned girl. And one thing is certain, that so long as the Yemen remains a closed country this traffic in slaves will continue. What's more, so long as Britain permits the cancerous sore of Sheikh Othman to fester in the desert, the supply of half-caste baby girls will go on," she told me, and I wondered if any of the thousands of British sailors who visited Sheikh Othman at the end of the war ever paused to think that their daughters may now be in a Yemenite harem or that their sons at this moment are probably satisfying the perverted lusts of some desert sheikh?

Chapter XI

I OBTAINED MY visa for Saudi Arabia in Khartoum before I was particularly interested in the slave trade. It is not an easy country to visit. Indeed, it might be said that strangers are actively discouraged. And unless one is a representative of one of the great oil companies there, endless difficulties are placed in one's way.

I first applied for a visa to Saudi Arabia when I was in Khartoum in 1957. I got nowhere. Three times, I was called before the authorities; the third time I was told that my application had been sent to Riyadh, but as it was the feast of Ramadhan there would be a delay before a reply was received. When I asked how long, my interviewer shrugged his shoulders and murmured: "Who knows? It may be a month, on the other hand, it may be two, *Inshallah* (as Allah wills)."

I discovered later when discussing my problem with some American tourists who were also trying to visit the country, that they had come up against the same difficulties. Apparently, such an evasive attitude was an old trick of the Saudis. If they wish to prevent a stranger entering their country they do not say so directly, for to do so would be a breach of Arab hospitality. Instead, they simply say that the application for a visa has been sent to Riyadh, and every time one visits them to inquire, one is given coffee and politely told that the reply has not yet been received. This farce may continue for months, until the exasperated applicant abandons his projected visit in despair.

Later, in 1957, I made another attempt to get a visa; this time in Addis Ababa. Diplomatic relations had just been established between Ethiopia and Saudi Arabia, and I thought that perhaps the members of the Saudi Embassy might not yet have had time to learn all the old tricks of procrastination. But they had, and some new ones as well.

"Who were your father and mother, and who were your grandfather and grandmother? Were any of them Jews?" I was asked.

Having answered these questions, I was then informed that my application would be forwarded to Riyadh. I spent the next two weeks calling at the Embassy, only to be told that my application had not yet been returned. After three weeks, I was ushered into the presence of the Ambassador himself.

"Your application has been approved," he told me, to my astonishment. "But I regret that as the Embassy has only just been established, we have no stamp with which to mark our official approval on your passport. We have applied for one to our capital."

"How long will it be before you receive it, your Excellency?" I asked, although I felt pretty certain that I knew the answer.

"Who knows? It may be a month. On the other hand, it may be two. *Inshallah*," he replied.

There the matter would have ended but for the fact that in 1956 while in Ataba in the Sudan, I had met a representative of one of the major oil companies, who was staying at the resthouse there. He was a Sudanese and had many friends in Saudi Arabia. I now told him what had happened and he immediately got in touch with somebody in Saudi Arabia. Wheels began to move, and a few days later, he told me to apply again to the Saudi Arabian Embassy, mentioning my previous application. When I returned to Khartoum, I did as he suggested.

The senior clerk at the Embassy asked me if I was willing to pay the cost of a telegram, prepaid, between Khartoum and Riyadh. Two days later, he telephoned me at my hotel to tell me that my visa was ready, and when I took my passport to them it was stamped without further ado.

I flew to Djeddah from Aden, looked up a friend in the oil

company, who introduced me to a number of prominent Saudi Arabian businessmen.

One evening over coffee I mentioned my interest in the slave trade to a Sudanese friend who had a business in Djeddah, telling him that I was collecting information for a book on the subject.

He looked at me with alarm. "Mr. John, I beg of you to forget all about slavery while you are in this country. It is a forbidden subject. In fact, it is more dangerous to talk about even than religion or politics. If the authorities found that you intended to write such a book, anything might happen to you."

"What do you mean by anything?" I asked, not taking his remark seriously.

"You don't know Saudi Arabia," he replied, dropping his voice. "It is a country where anything can happen. I beg of you to forget the whole thing," he added earnestly.

I imagine I must have looked unconvinced, for the Sudanese, who knew Saudi Arabia, insisted on delivering me a lecture on that country.

"You cannot even begin to understand this country until you know the meaning of the word Saudi," he told me. "It means that the Jedj, the Hasa, the Hejaz, and in fact all the other great desert wastes which make up this country belong personally to the King. He owns them all and every living creature that exists in them—including the slaves. Saudi Arabia is an absolute monarchy and King Saud Ibn Adulaziz el Saud is an absolute monarch. Those are facts that you should never forget so long as you are here," he warned.

I listened without comment to his warning, for I preferred to keep to myself the fact that I knew more about Saudi Arabia than he imagined. I knew, for instance, that the slave population was estimated at about 450,000 and that since the country had become rich through oil that population was rising. Because of this vast new wealth the price of slaves had soared and the slave trade had become a more profitable business than ever before. I knew that milky-skinned Sudanese girls fetched three hundred pounds apiece in the slave markets and that the slave traders' best customers were the three hundred and twenty-odd princes of the royal family, all of whom lived in luxury on pensions from the King.

I had set my heart upon seeing a slave market and so pressed my companion to take me to the Suk-el-Abid. He protested that he had never been there, but eventually admitted that he had a friend who knew where the place was. After a good deal of argument, I managed to extract a promise from him that he would introduce me to this friend.

A few evenings later the Saudi Arabian was brought to my hotel. He was a tall, fair-skinned man of about forty with an imposing and dignified presence. When he heard what I wanted to do, he strongly advised against it.

"As an Englishman, to be caught in such a place might be highly dangerous for you," he said.

I said as politely as I could that the more he tried to dissuade me the more determined I would be. After an hour of argument in a vile mixture of Arabic and English, I won the day, and the Saudi agreed to take me to the slave market for five hundred royals— fifty pounds. He explained that this sum was not all for himself as he would have to pay a dallal or auctioneer, who would make the necessary arrangements.

"Slave auctions are no longer held regularly," he told me, "except in an alley in Mecca, known as the Dakkat el Abeed— the slave platform. Elsewhere, the purchase of slaves is carried out by private treaty. In Djeddah now there are only five dallals, although there are many more in Riyadh and Mecca."

The next day the Saudi called at the hotel to tell me that the dallal was expecting a consignment of slaves after dark on the following Saturday.

"They will be sold on Sunday in the courtyard of his house," he explained. "I have arranged with him that you shall go to his house after nightfall on Saturday. You will go to a room overlooking the courtyard from which you can watch the auction. On Sunday night when it is again dark I will call for you. You must put on the Arab headgear of kefiyah and agal. Then with your sunburned face and your beard you will be able to pass as an Arab," he added.

"But what about my clothes?" I asked.

"They do not matter," he answered. "Today many Arabs among the educated classes wear western clothes. But remember if anyone should challenge you to answer in Arabic that you are a Jordanian."

It was after nine o'clock and quite dark when he called for me on Saturday night. As soon as we were well clear of the hotel, we turned into an alley and I put on the kefiyah and the agal he had brought for me. Then we walked quickly and in silence through the tortuous maze of streets and alleyways. Nobody seemed interested in us, for the shadowy night-prowlers, like lean tomcats, were preoccupied with their own nefarious business. Finally, we reached a narrow street and the Saudi in whispered Arabic told me that we were in the Suk-el-Abid where behind the high walls the slave auctions were held.

The door was opened to us by a shrouded sinister figure who proved to be the dallal.

"Ahlan," he greeted us. "Ahlan wa Sahlán." (You are welcome.)

He led us across the courtyard, up a narrow flight of stairs and along an evil-smelling passage to a little room. It was hot and airless, its small latticed window tightly shut, and the tired fan merely stirred the fetid air. I realised with a shudder that this was to be my home for the next twenty-four hours. Here I was to be a prisoner with nothing to cheer me except the flask of coffee and the few sandwiches I had brought with me.

As I moved to the window and looked down at the courtyard, the dallal explained that in the old days the room was used by important sheikhs visiting the Suk-el-Abid to buy slaves. Instead of demeaning himself by mixing with the common crowd in the street, he sat at the window to watch the slaves run, walk and lift weights from the window. The auction over, the slaves were brought to an adjoining room where the sheikh examined them privately and at his leisure.

"Here," the dallal told me, "you must keep still and remain

unseen, for to be heard or seen would be to risk your life."

Pointing to a dirty mattress with a wooden pillow, he said "There you will sleep." And with that, he and the Saudi left me. I heard the lock click, and knew that I was shut up in that wretched room for a day and a night.

It was one of the longest nights I have ever spent. The room was stifling and I discovered to my horror that the window was firmly bolted. Soon I was dripping with sweat, but there was neither water nor a towel. In desperation I stripped naked and lay down on the mattress, rolling my clothes into a pillow, for the wooden one provided for me was hardly conducive to sleep. Tossing and turning on the floor, I wondered whether I had been mad to start on such an adventure. Only the Saudi and the dallal knew that I had come to the house. Perhaps I had walked into a trap, and at some time during the night the door might open while I slept and I might be set upon by thugs. In such a house, it would be all too easy to disappear without trace.

Jumping to my feet with my heart pounding, I listened at the door. But the house was wrapped in silence. I do not know how long I had been asleep when I was awakened by shouts and screams coming from the courtyard. Rushing to the window, I looked down to see a dozen slaves being herded through a door at the far end of the yard. They were being driven in like cattle by three hefty guards armed with long-lashed whips. Even as I watched, one of the poor wretches, a Sudanese girl with huge breasts, received a savage lash across her naked buttocks with the curling lash, and let out a shriek of agony.

When the last of the slaves had been driven across the courtyard into a room below, I went back to my mattress and lay there unable to sleep, with the dreadful cries of the Sudanese girl ringing in my ears.

As the sunlight fell across the dusty floor, I heard a bustle of noise in the courtyard. I looked at my watch and was surprised to see that the time was nine o'clock. Climbing stiffly to my feet and stretching my aching limbs, I went to the window. Below, about thirty Arabs had gathered round a raised platform in the centre of the yard, and were sitting on their haunches chattering together. They were a motley collection. Some old, toothless and grey; others strikingly handsome in their flowing white robes, the gold thread woven into their headdresses glinting in the early morning sunlight.

As the dallal stepped on to the platform, they fell silent. For a good five minutes he harangued his audience, waving his arms and working himself, if not his listeners, into a fine state of excitement. Although I could not understand what he was saying, I guessed that he was extolling the virtues of his wares. When he had finished he gestured to the two Arabs who stood at the foot of the rostrum. Both were armed with cruel-looking whips.

I watched them go quickly to the door at the end of the court-yard to reappear leading a negro. He was a huge muscular man, and as naked as the day he was born. He walked with quiet dignity between the two guards onto the rostrum to stand glaring contemptuously at the crowd below him.

The dallal began shouting at his audience again, prodding the negro's flanks with a small stick and obviously stressing his magnificent strength.

The bidding began slowly, but soon the competition became brisk. One by one, the bidders became silent, until only two were left. One of them rose to his feet and spoke to the dallal, who stopped the auction while the negro descended from the rostrum and ran round the courtyard, his naked body gleaming like burnished copper in the brilliant sunlight. As the auctioneer called to him to halt, the two rival bidders examined him expertly. They ran their hands over his rippling muscles, ordered him to bend down with his head between his knees, sounded his huge chest, opened his mouth to look at his flashing teeth, and pinched his flesh. Then, as he climbed to the rostrum once .more, the bidding began again. I saw one of the Arabs throw up his hands in a gesture of despair as the dallal pointed his wand three times in the direction of his rival. It was for all the world as if he were saying: "Going! Going! Gone!" to the Arab in the black kefiyah whose dark eyes twinkled with triumph.

The negro was led away to be claimed by his new owner as soon as the price of his body had been handed over.

His place on the rostrum was taken by a negress. Like her predecessor, she was stark naked and probably about thirty-five years old. But unlike him, she struggled fiercely with her guards until she received a couple of lashes across her shoulders, which subdued her.

The audience showed little interest in her, and although the auctioneer shouted and screamed, making the woman turn this way and that, he failed to rouse their interest. They stood around in groups chatting idly amongst themselves, only occasionally glancing towards the naked woman on the platform. I found myself comparing them to a group of farmers at a fair, when a cow they suspect of being a bad milker is put up to auction.

In Saudi Arabia women of thirty-five are a drug on the slave market, useful only as house slaves, cleaners or domestic menials, and have little value. When a woman has reached the age of twenty she is sexually of little use and her owner will sell her for whatever price he can get in order to buy a girl of thirteen or fourteen to replace her. Thus, as a woman grows older she loses value each time she is sold. And by the time she has reached fifty she is virtually unsaleable, and is freed to beg or scavenge for her living. If she fails to make one, she dies miserably. *Inshallah*. It is the will of Allah.

At last one of the buyers made what must have been a very low bid for the negro woman, for the dallal began to tear his hair in despair. Then, a toothless old brute made another bid, and the auction went slowly on. But it struck me that they were all bidding derisively. At last, after much hair-tearing on the part of the dallal, the woman was knocked down to the old Arab to be led away and claimed later.

As the next slave was led in, a murmur of excitement went up amongst the buyers and they crowded closer round the rostrum.

He was a slender boy of about twelve years old with beautifully classical Arab features. Although much has been written about Arab brotherhood and solidarity, I knew that the Arab has no compunction in enslaving his fellows should they fall into his hands.

The boy was naked and tried to cover his privates with his little hands as he ran up the steps of the rostrum. As he stumbled in shy terror, the guards lifted him bodily up the steps.

Now the dallal had no need to hawk his wares, for the bidding was keen. All he had to do was to rub his wrinkled hands delightedly as the bidding soared.

The boy was a tender doe-eyed effeminate little creature with a soft round bottom, and it was all too clear from the expressions on the faces of the bidders why they wished to buy him. The majority of Arabs are bi-sexual; in fact, many of them have told me without a trace of shame that they prefer to share their couch with a young boy rather than a girl. Indeed, there is an age-old saying among the desert Bedouin: "A goat for use, a girl for enjoyment, but a boy for ecstasy."

Sickened with disgust, I watched several of the bidders examine the boy's buttocks minutely. And although I could not hear the bidding, judging by the wide smile on the dallal's evil face, I knew that the child must have been sold for a very high price. He was claimed by a tall, bearded Arab with full red lips, who led him from the rostrum with an arm around his waist. The child went without resistance for he was destined for a life of luxury and indulgence, at least until he grew too old to satisfy his master's desires.

The auction dragged on without enthusiasm until the last slave appeared. She was a half-caste girl of about fourteen with long black hair falling over her young breasts. Screaming hysterically, and fighting her guards like a tigress, she was dragged towards the platform. As one great brute held her wrists, the other lashed her across her bare buttocks until they were criss-crossed by fearful red weals so that I thought the tender drawn skin must split. The dallal, obviously fearful that such valuable property would be damaged, shouted at his guards to desist. But they did not hear him, so that he was forced to jump down from the rostrum and lay about the guards with his wand.

Even when they had dragged the child on to the platform, she still fought her captors so that they had to tie her arms behind her back. Only then did she submit to the close examination of the buyers.

For some reason only three Arabs bid for the girl, and all were called to the platform to inspect her. This they did thoroughly feeling her small breasts, running their hands down her wealed flanks, and forcing her legs apart in order to satisfy themselves that she was still a virgin.

The inspection over, the bidding began. It was conducted with less enthusiasm than for the boy, and the girl was finally knocked down to a grizzled old sheikh who must have been well into his seventies. It will be long before I shall forget the look of revulsion on that slave girl's face as the old man pawed her young body triumphantly after his bid had won her for him.

I was surprised when no further slaves appeared for it was only eleven o'clock and the auction had lasted but two hours. Nevertheless, in that space of time some six human beings had been disposed of like cattle. More important, I had seen with my own eyes the revolting but positive proof that slavery still flourished in Saudi Arabia, a country whose delegates to the United Nations never miss the opportunity to criticise the conduct of the Western countries. But the vast wealth that has come to Saudi Arabia from the oil spurting from her desert sands has done little or nothing to relieve the misery and poverty of her people. Syphilis is still rampant and trachoma still blinds countless Arab children in this country where the King and his nobles buy Cadillacs by the score and abandon them without thought in the desert when they break down. It is a fact that although there are only two hundred miles of paved roads in the country, Saudi Arabians bought more than two hundred and fifty Cadillacs in 1958. Most of these cars went to the three hundred and twenty-two princes supported by the King.

It is true to say that today the situation in Saudi Arabia is worse than it has ever been in the whole of its history. For today the inequality between the rich and the poor has reached scandalous proportions. Out of his oil royalties, King Saud has built himself no fewer than twenty-four palaces. To impress his guests at a banquet, he once ordered, from a Swiss jeweller, a silver table service weighing over a ton; a suite of mahogany furniture adorned with the royal coat-of-arms from a Lebanese cabinet-maker; and a Dresden service from Germany. The contracts for these orders were signed by one of the King's secretaries, who moistened his thumb with ink from an emerald and diamond encrusted fountain pen. But the King, who did not hesitate to spend £260,000 for a Bohemian crystal chandelier imported from Glassexport, still permits public executions in the streets of his capital, Riyadh, where it is a common sight to see a one-time thief walking abroad without hands. The executioner is the local butcher, and the heads and hands of his victims are hung from a telegraph pole where they remain for all to see, stinking to high heaven in the scorching sun.

All this and more I recalled as I sat waiting to be released from the stifling heat of my temporary prison overlooking the slave market. Late on that Sunday night when the dallal opened my door, I asked him what had become of the other slaves who were not sold at the auction. He answered that they had been sold en bloc to a wealthy slave dealer from Mecca, who would probably re-sell them at a considerable profit. He told me that the slave market, known as the Dakkat el Abeed, is in an alley in Mecca. In order to reach it, it would be necessary to pass the barrier some twenty-five miles outside Jedda, which bars the entrance to the Holy City to all non-Moslems. Thus does religious fanaticism hide from the outside world the hideous buying and selling of human souls in the open market in Saudi Arabia.

Chapter XII

THERE ARE NO two ways about an Arab's friendship, he either likes you or he hates your guts. He regards insincerity as a deadly sin; "two-faced" is an unknown word in his language. They are a demonstrative people; if they like you they show it openly, and have none of the "reserve" on which the Englishman prides himself. I think that is why the Irish and the Arab make a good combination; the Irish have little reserve either, a fact which the Arabs appreciate. I know one Irishman who has lived among them for thirty-five years. Except for the colour of his skin and the fact that he worships God in a different way he is completely Arab. He talks and thinks like an Arab. When I mentioned this to him one day he said, "What we in the West forget is that Arab thinking and the Arab way of life are completely different from ours, as different as the Sudanese from the Eskimo. We come to their countries and we expect them to be like us, or at least to conform to our pattern of behaviour. We try to impose a system, a class system, on a race which has no class. The Mohammedan religion specifically states that all men, that is all Arabs, are equal before God. Therefore the beggar in rags thinks he is every bit as good a man as the Sheikh. Their circumstances of life may be different, one has more wealth than the other, but man for man they are equal, and the Sheikh understands this as well as the beggar. It is only in these new rich oil countries that the idea has crept in that wealth makes one man better than another. When I was in Saudi Arabia recently I heard of the case of an oil Sheikh, a tremendously rich man. One day he was driving along the desert road in a large Cadillac, accompanied by his bodyguard. In front of them drove a schoolmaster in a vintage car. The Sheikh's driver overtook him rapidly, and gave a blast on his horn. Because the schoolmaster did not pull off the road immediately the Sheikh's driver stopped the car, his two bodyguards alighted, pulled the unfortunate schoolmaster from his car and beat him up badly. They then set fire to his car. Now, this would never have happened in the old days when the Sheikh would probably have ridden a camel and the schoolmaster a donkey."

I asked him how he regarded the slave trade.

"Like every other humane man I loathe it," he answered, "but we must look at it from the Arab's point of view. He is a proud man, too proud to do any menial work. From time immemorial there were slaves for that type of work, and as long as the Arab has money to buy them he will do so. All our resolutions at the United Nations will not stop him. I was in Arabia when the late King Ibn Saud issued the decree concerning slavery in 1936. You know the one, entitling the slave to good food, good clothing, medical attention, etc., etc. It was all eyewash for Western consumption. Arabs went on treating their slaves exactly as they had done before. The good Arabs, and they are in the vast majority, always treated their slaves well. After all, they are valuable property for which their owners paid good money. Why lessen their market value by flogging them severely or half starving them? Would you beat or half starve a thoroughbred horse or a prize bull? It might have been all right in the old days, when slaves were plentiful and cheap, but today they are an expensive commodity, and must be well looked after."

I got a similar viewpoint from an Arab, none other than the dallal who held the auction I had witnessed. I had had little opportunity of speaking to him on the night I left the house, just a few words of thanks and a hurried handshake. A couple of days later he sent the Saudi with an invitation to me to visit his house for coffee. He apparently liked me, and felt that the traditional rule of Arab hospitality, the drinking of coffee together, had been broken. He was again waiting for me at the door, a lean, hawk-nosed old rogue, with a permanent twinkle in his eye, as if always amused at some inward joke.

On this occasion I was led to a ground floor room. It was clean, bare, and wonderfully cool. We squatted, Arab fashion, on the rugs spread on the floor. A slave boy, a good looking well-built lad of about sixteen, brought in the coffee pot and cups. He looked to be half Arab and half Negro, probably the son of a negro woman by an Arab father, who because his mother was a slave, would remain a slave all his life.

The dallal, the Saudi and I drank our coffee in silence, as is required by Arab custom, making loud smacking noises with our lips to show our appreciation. Then the dallal turned to me and said in Arabic, "And now I will sell you a slave." I wondered if I had heard aright. He spoke a form of Arabic similar to that spoken by the Senegalese in Djibouti, which I found rather difficult to follow.

"What did he say?" I asked the Saudi, who spoke English.

"He asked you if you would buy a slave."

"I thought that was what he asked, but what the hell would I do with a slave?"

The Saudi laughed. "Better ask him yourself," he said, "and tell him to speak more slowly as your Arabic is not good."

When I did so the old dallal said: "Every white man wants a slave," adding, "he wants to take her back to his own country as evidence of our brutality and backwardness. Think what a sensation it would cause in your country when you arrived with a slave. Everybody would say what savages we in Saudi Arabia are. Your Government would probably start a war on Saudi Arabia, to free the poor slaves, as they started a war on Egypt to protect British lives and property."

"They are not my God-damned Government," I answered heatedly, "I . . ."

It was then that I realised he was having me on, taking the mickey out of me.

"All right, all right," he chuckled, "I knew you were not an Englishman, my friend here told me. We do not like the English for what happened in Suez. They pretended to make war to protect lives and property, and all the time they were helping the Jews."

I found this idea firmly held by all the Arabs in the Middle East and no amount of arguing can change their opinions. "But I did not bring you here to talk politics," he went on. "My friend told me you are going to write about the slave trade. When you do so please write the truth. Many people write who do not know anything about it. They make us out to be monsters. You will write in any case, and I cannot prevent you, so I show you my auction that you may see for yourself we are not monsters, but honest men, trying to make a living in these difficult days."

"What about the young girl I saw flogged?" I asked.

"Ah, she was a wild one. I was a fool to buy her, but she was very cheap and I was tempted. She is a Syrian, stolen from her village and smuggled into the country a few days previously. She had not settled down yet, and a taste of the whip is always necessary in such cases. Believe me I regret the necessity as much as anybody. It is not good to have the buttocks wealed, it lowers the market value. Besides, she was not a virgin; they start young, these Syrians."

"Is there any truth in the stories I have heard about pilgrims to Mecca from the Sudan or French Equatorial Africa being seized and sold?" I asked.

"It seldom happens nowadays," he answered, "except of course if a pilgrim from another land breaks the law of our country like—" and here he grinned broadly—"landing on our coast without a permit."

I had heard of this racket in Khartoum, perhaps the most unscrupulous of all methods of obtaining slaves. Moslems from French Equatorial Africa or the Sudan make the long, weary journey to the coast, often on foot, their worldly possessions carried by a solitary camel. I had seen some of them the previous year pass through Atbara, making their way to Port Sudan or Suakin. They have never heard of passports or visas. Arriving at the ports, they find that they cannot sail without a visa or travel document. As the greatest ambition of any Moslem's life is to make the pilgrimage to Mecca, they are bitterly disappointed. However, at Suakin a dhow's captain is always ready to oblige them by smuggling them across to the Saudi Arabian coast, for whatever fee they can afford. If they have no money he, being a true Moslem, offers to take them anyhow. They are put ashore on the Saudi Arabian coast, and told that a guide will be along presently to lead them to Mecca. After some time a guide does show up, and after obtaining as much money as he can extract from the unfortunate pilgrims does guide them, straight into the arms of waiting policemen. They are arrested for being on Saudi Arabian soil without a permit, and hustled off to jail. After being kept there for a couple of weeks, half starved and often beaten, word is sent to some of the important Sheikhs who want slaves that such and such a number are available in the jail. They arrange to visit the prison, and point out the people they require. The prisoners are then informed that a kind man is willing to pay the exorbitant, and mythical, fine which was imposed on them, provided that they are prepared to work for him. In all cases they agree; anything to get away from the horror of the prison. They are now slaves and remain so for the rest of their lives.

Another method of obtaining slaves, also practised in the name of religion, is for an important Moslem to take his wives and female servants on a pilgrimage to Mecca. He returns, probably six months later, minus a couple of wives and the female servants. To any inquiries he simply answers that the wives decided to remain on in Mecca. Naturally they had to have servants to attend them. I remember once flying from Khartoum to Port Sudan on a pilgrims' aircraft of Sudan Airways bound for Djeddah. I happened on that occasion to be in a hurry to reach Port Sudan, and my good friend, the publicity manager of Sudan Airways, found me a seat on this plane. I noticed several of the Moslem pilgrims travelling with large retinues of women, and I wondered how many of them would return to the Sudan.

Before leaving the dallal's house he again pressed us to have coffee, served this time by a smiling Arab boy. I remarked, half jokingly, that his slaves at any rate seemed happy enough.

"Believe me," he answered earnestly, "we in Saudi Arabia treat our slaves well. After all, to us they are a valuable commodity. Slaves are becoming more expensive every year. Would you ill-treat a valuable horse you had paid a lot of money for? Of course there are exceptions, there are bad men in every country, but on the whole they are treated as one of the family, and often rise to positions of trust in the household. Put that in your book."

I was reminded of the planter who, just before the pro-mulgation of the French Emancipation decree of 1848, published a pamphlet in which he stated that slavery was a benefit to all blacks and a burden to the whites. He added that if the masters were armed with whips it was to caress paternally the laggards and the idlers!

PART II

SLAVERY TODAY IN AFRICA AND ARABIA

Chapter I

BEFORE GOING ON to my own study of slave trading and slave-owning in Saudi Arabia in all its brutal details perhaps it would be as well to look at the opinions of others on the subject, people who, by virtue of residence in Saudi Arabia, had more ample opportunity of studying the whole trade at first hand. It should be emphasised that these people were not mere "do-gooders" and that their writings are not the vapourings of "misguided sentimentalists."

In 1925 the Temporary Slavery Commission set up by the League of Nations had this to say:

"Information from reliable sources enables the commission to state that the slave trade is practised openly in several Mohammedan States of Asia and in particular in the Hedjaz."

It further stated that African slaves intended for the markets of Saudi Arabia obviously embarked from territories belonging to Egypt, the Sudan, Eritrea, the French Somali coast, British Somaliland or Italian Somaliland. It further stated that the Hashimite Government received dues on slaves sold in the markets which "is the equivalent to an official recognition of the legality of this trade." It went on, "We are informed on authority which is regarded as entirely trustworthy that many of the slaves of foreign origin in the Hedjaz are either young girls from the Far East who come as pilgrims or are smuggled in for sale; or are persons coming from various countries accompanying their parents or masters in the pilgrimage to Mecca. The former case would seem to merit the attention of the Commissions concerned with the traffic in women, but there appears no doubt that they are sold as slaves."

Dr. Paul Harrison, an American medical missionary, spent fourteen years in Arabia, and had first-hand knowledge of the slave trade. In his book, *The Arab at Home*, he writes, "As might be expected, these true believers do not consider themselves recipients of special favour because they are God's favourites. The conclude that they are actually the cream of the universe, essentially better than all other beings, demons, angels or men, because they have signified their acceptance of a philosophical concept. Such men want no instruction from the despised and contemptible infidel on subject secular or religious. The pride and the intolerance thus developed can scarcely be matched in the world, and an almost immovable stagnation of society results. This intolerance and stagnation are made worse by the fact that Mohammedanism tends to place all ethical values on outward appearances and ritual observances and ignores the motives that lie underneath. Religion comes to be a set of forms to be gone through. They may be sincerely performed, but they have little value in shaping the character, because they make no demand on the worshipper's conscience."

A second inconsistency similar to the intolerant persecution of the infidels is the inclusion of slavery in the Mohammedan system. Scarcely anything could be imagined more opposed to the genius of Mohammedanism than for one believer to be held as a chattel slave of another. To keep an infidel as a slave might be open to less theoretical objections, but as a matter of fact the slaves are all Mohammedans, indeed they are almost compelled to be. A pious Mohammedan takes great pains with the religious education of his slaves, especially of the slave children.

It is interesting to discuss the institution of slavery with earnest Mohammedans. Their progressive leaders frequently admit that slavery is inconsistent with the solidarity of Mohammedanism and apologise for it. Men of that type, however, are uncommon and such opinions are expressed in private. In public the institution enjoys all the prestige that entrenched privilege enjoys everywhere and any criticism of it in the gathering of the rich and the great calls forth the same horrified protests that the beneficiaries of Bolshevism would produce in a Wall Street office. Religion endorses it, the social order depends upon it and the welfare of the slaves themselves demands it. The Sheikh of Abu Dahbi once spent the best part of half an hour explaining to me that the slaves who were freed lived under conditions far worse in every way than those they had enjoyed while still slaves. The secret visitors who came at night to my room asking for assistance in running away did not hold his opinion. Indeed, the poor fishermen of Bahrein have a clearer view on the matter. It is not hard for them to see that slavery is an iniquity. Moreover, Mohammedanism itself in a curious way recognises the evil of the system and makes it an act of great religious merit to purchase a slave and free him. This is frequently done and all Arab towns along the coast have their contingent of freed slaves.

Of slavery in Saudi Arabia, Eldon Rutter, at a lecture to the Central Asia Society, spoke of a visit to Mecca.

"We do not come as pilgrims but as investigators of slavery. We therefore take particular note of a score or so of tall negroes in immense turbans who are standing or walking near the house of Allah. These men are called Aghas. They are eunuch slaves and are employed as police in the great Mosque. There are about fifty of them altogether, and their duties are not very heavy. They were first established in the Mosque in the eighth century. They are employed because squabbling women have at times to be ejected. No man is supposed to touch a woman who is not his wife or closely related to him, but a eunuch is not classed as a man in the proper sense of the word. Most of the Aghas have been presented to the Mosque by Mohammedan princes. Nowadays they are chiefly purchased as boys by the chief Agha. They are not owned by any person, but are slaves of Allah. They are in fact presumptuously presented to God by their fellow men, a sort of bloodless human sacrifice; the last thing they would be likely to desire would be their freedom from this to them honourable and prosperous slavery."

The streets and precincts are full of slaves, some well dressed and carrying daggers, who escort their masters as bodyguards. We see, too, a few old slave women. They are recognisable by the poverty of their clothing and the lack of proper veils, but we see nothing of the several thousands of younger women slaves who are kept close in the shuttered houses of the city.

We make our way through the dusty ways which surround the mosque, and presently come into a narrow street called the Suk-el-Abid. It is very narrow, and the tall houses on either side allow very little daylight to reach the roadway. Against these houses there are stone benches resembling the display counters of shops and so, indeed, they are, for these houses are the shops of dealers in human beings. The slaves are sitting on the benches— some silent, others talking together, some even joking and laughing. The most desirable of the slave girls are not exposed to view. They are kept inside the houses, where prospective buyers are taken in to view them. There are also street auctioneers called dallal; among the dallal are a number who specialise in the sale of slave girls, and they conduct the buyers to the house where the slaves may be inspected. The best slaves are sold among the citizens by private treaty in this way. As we move along in the cloisters we see two or three very old men and women who look like dreary black skeletons. If we go to the mosque at sunrise we shall see some of these. If we go at sunset they will be there too, and if we pass by at midnight we shall see them there still, sleeping on the stones in their rags. They have no home but the mosque, and no food but what they receive in alms; turned out to seek the bounty of Allah, as their masters would say.

Perhaps the most damning indictment of slavery in Saudi Arabia is contained in a dispatch from the French Ambassador in Saudi Arabia to the French Government. Here it is:

"Djeddah
7th November, 1953
"The Ambassador of France at Djeddah to H.E. the Minister of Foreign Affairs, Division of the Near East.

"If the presence of slaves in Saudi Arabia and the trade in negroes carried off from their native land by many tricks to be sold among the rich inhabitants of Mecca, of Rijadh or of Djeddah, are well-known facts it is not easy, however, to assemble complete written evidence on this question, on account of the highly clandestine character of their acquisition. Thanks to investigations carried out in the heart of the Senegalese colony at Djeddah, I have nevertheless been able to get together a certain amount of information, of which the exactness of the details, combined with the agreement between the evidence of the witnesses support their authenticity.

"Merchants living in Djeddah or Mecca send naturalised Saudi Arabians but of Senegalese origin for the most part, as emissaries commissioned to recruit a number of people from the villages of the Sudan of the High-Volta or of the Niger; Timbuctoo in particular is often visited by these malign persons. They pose as Muslim missionaries entrusted with the delicate mission of guiding their compatriots to the Holy Places of Islam to make the pilgrimage and to be instructed in the Koran in Arabic. A number of Moslem natives fall into this trap. Men, women and children are then transported under the guidance of their kind guides to the shores of the Red Sea at Port Sudan or Suakin; the journey is made, it seems, by lorry, thanks to local assistance. Having crossed the Red Sea in specially chartered dhows, the negroes disembark at Rith, a little port 200 kilometres south of Djeddah. There they are declared to be illicit pilgrims, are loaded into lorries and transported to Djeddah where they are put in prison. Their stay there lasts only a short time. Next day a Saudi Arabian merchant arrives, and receives from the hands of the police delivery of his merchandise. Immediately sold, the unfortunate people are taken to the houses of their masters which they will never leave as free men. The price of a slave varies naturally with its sex and age. A girl under fifteen years old is worth it seems, from 200,000 to 400,000 francs (£200 to £400); a man under forty is sold for 1,500 riyals (150,000 francs—£150); an old woman for 400 riyals (£40).

These sales are usually carried out by brokers in the markets. All evidence points to the slaves being well treated. On condition that they accept their lot, renounce all idea of freedom, and submit body and soul to the desires of their masters, they are assured of a material existence well superior to that which they could get in their village in Africa. The men can rise to posts of trust, such as steward, chauffeur, bodyguard, etc. The women who become mothers are treated in practice as wives. I have been able to get the names of the principal traders in slaves from French Africa. They are Amadov Bouboue, a Senegalese, naturalised Saudi Arabian, resides at Djeddah; Sheikh Abdo Bagne, a native of the Niger, resides at Djeddah; Sheikh Abdallah Bouheirie, a Saudi Arabian, head of the municipality of Djeddah and representative (Ouakil) of the "Moutaouefs" guides of the pilgrims to Mecca, who sells slaves directly to the Princes; Omar Conde, a naturalised Senegalese, resides at Mecca; Hedj Manamadou Ba dit Omar Foutiov, a Senegalese, travels between French West Africa and Djeddah; Thierno Yero Ba, travels between French West Africa and Djeddah; Hadj Bely, a Senegalese, naturalised as a Saudi Arabian, travels between Rijadh and Mecca; Mohamed Taher, a distinguished Targui, resides in the French Sudan, travels between the Sudan, Timbuctoo, Cairo and Djeddah; Muhsan, a native of French Equatorial Africa, an employee of the American Baker Co., at Djeddah.

"No precise calculation is possible as to how many of the natives of French West and Equatorial Africa are thus sold annually as slaves. It seems to me that the total may not be very considerable, a few hundred perhaps. Meanwhile the natives of French Africa continue to be the greatest number of recruits to slavery in Arabia, recruitments in a slave-owning country being it seems much more difficult. The local demand continues to be strong. Slaves constitute an important element in the social organisation; the pride of the Arab hinders him from performing a number of tasks considered to be servile and degrading. So, with the connivance of the Saudi Arabian authorities the ancient trade in black ivory is perpetuated in our time in spite of the international conventions and of the fact that King Ibn Saud had adhered to the U.N. The paradox reached its summit following the recent speech of the Saudi Arabian Delegate to the U.N. on the question of Tunisia. A nation which tolerates on its soil the sale of human beings— French natives under the circumstances—whose religious sentiments have been exploited without scruple, seems far from well placed to attack France in the name of the Rights of Man."

Chapter II

WHAT CAUSES THE Arabs, more than any other race, to regard slavery as an essential part of their lives, and to hold slaves long after every other race has abolished the system?

There are many reasons, of which perhaps the religious, economic and sexual ones are the principal. There is nothing in the Mohammedan religion against the holding of slaves. Indeed, it may be said to encourage the enslavement of his fellow men by the Mohammedan. While the Mohammedan religion teaches that all men are strictly equal in the sight of Allah, rich man and poor, Sheikh and beggar, it is interpreted by the Arab as meaning that all Arabs are equal. The "outsider" is therefore the legitimate prey of every Arab—infidels and outcasts have no other purpose in life but to serve the Mohammedan. Therefore it is a noble and indeed a holy thing to take the infidel, the Sudanese, the Ethiopian or the native of the Belgian Congo or French Equitorial Africa as slaves. Although they are sometimes converted to Mohammedanism this does not place them on a par with the Arab, or give them any more rights than they had before.

There is also a very good economic reason for slavery. After the initial purchase price has been paid a slave costs nothing except his food, which is often extremely meagre, and the clothes he manages to pick up. The Arab system is a patriarchal one, the Sheikh as head of the tribe likes to be surrounded by as many slaves as possible as evidence of his importance. This is particularly true of the desert tribes of Bedouin. The slaves are for the most part kindly treated; no man is going to destroy valuable property by flogging him to death or mutilating him, although cases have been known where an Arab's rage has got the better of his sense of value, and a slave has been killed for a trifling offence. Running away is regarded as the most serious offence a slave can commit, and for that he is mercilessly flogged. For a second offence his private parts are removed, he is skewered to stakes in the desert, and there left to die a horrible lingering death. His testicles are then hung outside the Sheikh's tent, as a warning to other would-be runaways. Slaves are regarded as property and when a Sheikh dies the slaves are divided equally between his sons. In his book *The Arab at Home* Dr. Paul Harrison writes of slavery as an economic factor. "It is a great temptation, this opportunity to have one's work done by slaves, and nothing could seem to offer greater profits. The slaves have no rights. They can be punished if they show less diligence than their owner thinks adequate. They receive no wages at all, only such food and clothing as their master sees fit to give them. Arabs are not the only people who have been deceived by this fallacy. We believed it ourselves a hundred years ago. It has been a disastrous policy from every standpoint."

Nevertheless, the demand for slaves in the Yemen and Arabia is an ever increasing one. Prices are higher than ever before, and the new wealth that oil has brought to Saudi Arabia has enabled the oil-wealthy Sheikhs to purchase more and more slaves, displaying them as rich men in the West display pedigree cattle or thoroughbred horses.

This is particularly true of women slaves. Here the Arab's appetite is insatiable, and as more and more revenue from oil pours into the country, the wealthy Saudi-Arabians are able to purchase more and more women. Again, there is nothing in the Mohammedan religion to forbid the Arab to have as many women as he desires. True, he is only allowed four wives, but there is no limit to the number of concubines he may take, although Mohammed counselled moderation in all things. He may even divorce his wives and take new ones every day if he feels like it, by simply saying to them, "I divorce thee," three times.

Of this Doctor Harrison writes:

"Mohammedanism may fairly claim to have triumphed over race prejudices, and to have created the greatest internationalism in the world. It has triumphed over social and religious inequality and stands forth as a casteless system. But its triumph is illusory and its whole conception of a democratic society is rendered practically valueless by the fact that the female half of the population holds almost the status of pariahs with practically no rights at all. The appetites and passions of men have triumphed over the philosophy of Mohammedanism, and the conquest has been complete. Women are recognised as possessing souls and may hope for a place in Heaven; there is no theoretical reason for considering them essentially inferior to men. But their position has not been fixed with reference to the religious philosophy of the Arab, it has been fixed by the strength of the lusts of his flesh. . . .

"The Mohammedan system is nothing more nor less than unchecked promiscuity. It is true that the Bedouin community has remained monogamous in Arabia, but unfortunately it is the indulgence of the oasis rather than the monogamy of the desert that tends to be carried by the system. Consequently, women have no rights. A little girl may be married to a man of sixty. Her place is an inferior one, and she is frequently beaten. Her duty is obedience, no matter how weak-minded her husband or how impossible his demands. A few indulgent fathers have their daughters taught to read the Koran, but it would be fatal to a woman's reputation to know how to write. She might write a letter to some one other then her own husband. Infraction of the moral code is for her a capital crime. For the man it is a minor offence. There are exceptions, and again it is in the desert that we usually find them, but taken as a whole, family life in Arabia is a very unlovely thing to see. The husband dominates over his wife. She is his plaything, almost his slave. She is divorced at her husband's whim, whereas only grave reason and legal process enable her to divorce him. . . .

"The essence of this great evil of Mohammedanism is not in unlimited divorce nor even in polygamous relationships, but rather in that unqualified naturalism which the system teaches and which is universal in Arabia among Bedouins as well as all other Arabs. The relations of the sexes are reduced to the level of eating and drinking. A man enjoys a new sort of potato every day, why should he not enjoy a new wife every day?"

This attitude is responsible for the Arab's desire for slave women from many lands as concubines, a desire which men like the Egyptian, the Ethiopian, the Greek and the Yemenite endeavour to satisfy. White girls are the most eagerly sought after; a wealthy Arab will pay up to one thousand five hundred pounds for a white girl slave to satisfy this desire, and will travel to the Lebanon each year where white girls may be had in the brothels. In 1957, before the civil war broke out there, a scandal concerning this indulgence of some Saudi Arabians' whims rocked the Government. It was discovered that a brothel, of which the then Minister of Justice was reported to be part owner, was being run especially for wealthy oil Sheikhs. The "inmates" were high school girls between the ages of thirteen and sixteen, who set off for school each morning, but made their way to this brothel. Here they entertained the oil Sheikhs to every conceivable form of sexual perversion, performing singly, in pairs, and in whole groups. It was stated that the Madame who ran the establishment charged the Sheikhs one hundred and fifty pounds for a day's entertainment.

Next to white girls, the Arabs prefer negresses, particularly in summer. The reason is that in summer the negress's skin keeps cool, unlike her Arab or white sister's. She is also very prolific —a fact very dear to the Arab heart, as the female children of slave women remain slaves, and can be sold for a substantial amount, so that instead of paying for his pleasure, an Arab's pleasure pays him.

In this connection it is interesting to note a system which prevails in Mecca. Hundreds of Mohammedan students go there every year to study theology. They are usually too poor to buy a girl, so the benevolent slave dealers there give them a girl with whom they may live, charging a fee for her use. As all her children are born slaves, this "generosity" shows a handsome profit for the dealer, who sells the children. When the student has finished his studies he goes home, and the girl is rented to another student. So it goes on until she becomes too old for childbearing, and is set free, to join the army of scarecrows who hang round the cloisters of the mosque. This ensures the dealer a high place in Heaven, as the freeing of a slave was enjoined by Mohammed as a meritorious act.

Chapter III

THE SUDAN HAD been the happy hunting ground for slavers from the beginning of the last century, when the Ottoman Empire pushed its way southward, overrunning the native tribes.

In 1876, when Gordon was made Governor of all the Sudan, it was estimated that at least seven-eighths of the population were slaves. At that time slavery was big business, the revenue from it far exceeding that from ivory. Some of the European settlers in the Sudan at that time gave up their trading posts in disgust; others turned enthusiastically to the new and more profitable venture. They employed Arabs to capture and transport the slaves, while they arranged for their sale.

The Arabs and native rulers were not slow to cash in on this new venture. Indeed one of them, Zobeir, founded his own slave empire, with its capital at Darfur. So powerful did he become that the Governor who ruled the Sudan before Gordon begged Cairo to send an expedition against him. Instead, the authorities in Cairo invited him to the capital, where he was made a Pasha. In 1877 he was sent at the head of an Egyptian force to help the Turks in their fight against the Russians.

He was never allowed to return to Darfur. His son, Suliman, later led a rebellion against Gordon, by whom he was decisively defeated.

When Gordon took over the Governorship of the Sudan it was estimated that every Egyptian owned on an average one slave. Many wealthy families had hundreds of slaves. Some were well treated, but the majority were treated as were slaves in the days of the Roman emperors. Human life was cheap and the Arab slavers took full advantage of the fact.

When the slavers attacked a village nobody was spared. The old men and young children were butchered, the old and middle-aged women were brutally tortured to make sport for the slavers and then killed, while the young boys and girls were shackled together by the necks. After looting the village the raiders set fire to the huts. Then the long trek to the coast started. Chained together, half crazy with hunger and thirst, the slaves were driven towards the sea by the brutal whips of the Arab slave-traders. Between 1875 and 1879 Gordon estimated that 100,000 people were taken into slavery in the Sudan. The old slave roads to the coast, bestrewn by the skulls and bones of the poor creatures who perished, are their only monument.

The conditions of the slaves at this time was one of the utmost misery. In a letter dated 31st March 1879 at Edowa, Gordon says "This evening a party of seven slave dealers with twenty-three slaves were brought to me. Nothing could exceed the misery of these poor wretches. They had come across the torrid desert from Shaka, a journey from which I, on my camel, shrink. I got the slave dealers chained at once, the men and boys were put in the ranks, the women were told off to be the wives of soldiers, and the children were sent to Obeid, where I have established a settlement for them. When I had begun this letter another caravan with two slave dealers and seventeen slaves was brought in, and I heard others were on the way. Some of the women were quite nude. I have disposed of them in the same way, for what else can I do? Both of these caravans come from Shaka where I mean to make a clean sweep of the slave-dealers." (Shaka was the stronghold of Zobeir, and since his removal to Egypt, was ruled by his son Suliman.) "These captures make the total of caravans captured since July 1878 as sixty-three."

In another letter dated June 1878, Gordon wrote "As I write these words another caravan, consisting of eighteen slaves, had been captured, with two children. They were such skeletons. In less than two days I have caught seventy. There is no doubt that they have been passing at the rate of seventy a day for the last year or so."

Next day he wrote in his Journal. "We started this morning at 1 a.m. and halted at 7 a.m. Soon after we caught nine slave dealers, twenty slaves, and two donkeys. Some of these poor slaves were mere skeletons. No female child, however young, passes unscathed by these scoundrels. The law does not permit death to these scoundrels, so all I can do is to strip and flog them and send them like Adam into the desert. Next day at Tiashig we captured a hundred dealers and five hundred slaves." This expedition saved one thousand seven hundred slaves.

Gordon was tireless in his efforts not only to hunt down the slave traders, but to ameliorate the lot of the slaves. In a decree issued when he became Governor of the Sudan he ordered that slavery in the Sudan should be abolished within twelve years, but from the date he took over as Governor-General all Europeans had to give their slaves a paper of enfranchisement, and had in future to employ only free men. This decree was bitterly resented by the slave owners, European and Arab alike, and many intrigues were set on foot to get rid of Gordon. He survived them all and continued with his work of freeing slaves, until a Dervish spear in his throat ended his life in the red ruins of Khartoum.

At Gordon's death slavery again became rampant in the Sudan. Indeed, on the very day of the fall of Khartoum the slavers were busy. Every able-bodied man left alive after the sack of the city was pressed into service with the Dervish army, or became a slave to an Emir. The women were gathered into two zareba, white women in one, black women in another and the Emirs had their pick. From that day until the defeat of the Dervish army at Omdurman slavery had its hey-day in the Sudan. Barbarous cruelties were practised on the slaves. They were often made to take the places of beasts of burden in the armies of the Madhi. A revolt of slaves was put down ruthlessly, every one of them being put to death by being burned alive. Many fled and the tortures of the recaptured slave beggars description. Of the number who got away many joined the native ranks of Kitchener's army and fought in that fateful battle of Omdurman on 2nd December 1898, a battle that broke the power of the Dervish army, and ended organised slavery under the British in the Sudan. But an old custom dies hard; as supplies dwindled, prices rose, so that even today there are men in the Sudan prepared to sell their fellow human beings into slavery for the high prices they will fetch.

Chapter IV

WHILE IN DJEDDAH I made an application to visit the capital at Riyadh. I knew there was no possibility of getting permission to visit Mecca; few whites are permitted to go there, except on essential business. I was asked to return in two days time. When I did so I was called into the office of the Chief of Police and closely questioned as to my reason for visiting Riyadh. I explained that I was employed by a publishing firm producing a book on commerce and travel in the Middle East, and said I was interested in meeting the merchants to discuss the commercial possibilities there. "Are you sure that is all you are interested in writing about?" he asked, glancing at me searchingly.

"That's all, sir," I answered.

"Then, perhaps this may help you," he said, handing me a large volume, a directory of trade in Saudi Arabia. One part was in English, the other in Arabic, and it was produced by a firm in Saudi Arabia, and dedicated to His Gracious Majesty, King Ibn Saud, etc., etc. The English section simply contained photographs of the King and all his Ministers, sons, cousins, nephews; a whole section was devoted to advertising the various firms in Saudi Arabia. I learned later from the Sudanese that it was a very profitable venture; the publishers simply approached each firm and said, "We are producing a commercial directory, which will contain ten portraits of His Majesty and other Ministers. We know you will support it by advertising." The various firms knew better than to refuse. A hundred pounds a page was charged, and as it contained a hundred pages of advertising, everybody, with the possible exception of the advertisers, was happy, and the advertisers kept their unhappiness to themselves. I took the book from the Police Chief, and was about to thank him for his help when he said, "Application refused. Have you finished your business here in Djeddah?"

"Yes, sir," I answered.

"In that case, there is a plane leaving for Amman tomorrow morning. I suggest you are on it. Good-day."

I shall never know if he knew anything of my visit to the Suk-el-Abid, or if he was just naturally nasty. There are police spies and informers everywhere in Saudi Arabia, and one of them may have dropped a hint. Anyhow I thought it much safer to be on that plane the following day.

From Amman I went to Beirut, and from there to Teheran in Persia. There is no actual slavery in Persia, but I was told by a friend there that men are still shipped from Abadan to Kuwait by dhow captains who pretend to be able to find them work. Once arrived there they are smuggled on to Bahrein where they are sold as slaves. This was verified in the Iran Press while I was there. In November, 1958, two men in an emaciated condition were found on a deserted island in the Persian Gulf. They told their rescuers that they were the only two remaining alive out of a cargo of forty men and boys. They had been inveigled aboard a dhow at Abadan by a captain who promised that he would smuggle them into Kuwait, where they would find plenty of work. While at sea they were sighted by a ship of the Persian Navy. The captain immediately ran for it, and, eluding his pursuers, dumped his unfortunate passengers on an uninhabited island. Ten days later when they were discovered, thirty-eight had succumbed to hunger and thirst. When they had recovered, the men said that the captain had promised them plenty of work in Kuwait. When they got there they would probably have been told that a mistake had been made, the work was actually in Bahrein. Another man would take over, and they would be smuggled to Bahrein to work on the pearl diving boats. Here they are loaned money at exorbitant interest. They are encouraged to spend it, and when the Arab owners of the diving boats know it is all gone they ask for its return together with the interest. The debtor is unable to repay it, and offers to work it off. As an exorbitant interest is added each year he virtually becomes a slave, getting a little money each season, but never enough to repay the ever mounting debt.

Of this system Dr. Paul Harrison in his book the *Arab at Home* writes: "The diver is now a slave for the rest of his life. It is probably easier for a negro slave on the pirate coast to escape than it is for a Bahrein diver to regain his freedom. As long as he is in debt he cannot change his employer, no matter how badly he is treated, nor can he leave the town except under bonds to return before the diving season begins. And he will never be able to get out of debt. He cannot read or write. There is no witness to the transactions that take place between the captain and himself. It is the recognised thing for divers to receive a loan of rice when the season begins, so that their families may have something to eat while the head of the house is away. The sum written into the books is regularly about fifty per cent greater than the market price of the rice. If necessary, entirely false entries are written in. The upshot of the matter is that these men never get out of debt, not one in a thousand of them. In seven years residence in Bahrein, I have never yet met a diver who has 'escaped from the account book,' as the Arabs put it."

Further south, in Trucial Oman, slavery pure and simple exists. Here as in Saudi Arabia the Sheikhs are rich men and can afford to buy slaves, even at the high prices prevailing today. They derive their riches mainly from the date plantations and from the huge sums paid for concessions by the oil companies, in addition to the revenues paid by the merchants, shopkeepers and, on the coast, fishermen and pearl-fleet owners. Another profitable source of revenue is the sale of slaves to the pearl-fleet owners. All wrong-doers and criminals convicted of minor crimes are dealt with in this way. For a serious crime such as theft, the criminal's right hand is cut off in public in the market place; if the amount stolen is large the thief is publicly decapitated.

For the slave who tries to escape there is the punishment of the hooks. Sharp hooks are driven into a wall and the slave is taken to the top. He is then dropped on to the hooks and becomes impaled on them. He is left there to die slowly, as a warning to other slaves.

It will be remembered that Britain has treaty relations with these slave-owning sheikhs. Why, then, is nothing done to stop the trade in human beings, in an area where by virtue of the fact that the sheikhs are getting richer every year the vile trade is increasing? I believe the answer is a political one. The slave-owning sheikhs must be prevented at any cost from following the example of the Yemen, and throwing in their lot with Nasser and the United Arab Republic. These territories, as well as being a potential source of huge petroleum supplies are strategically of extreme importance to the British, and so the slave-owning Sheikhs must be cosseted. In the airport lounge in Aden I once saw a Political Officer fussing around one of these Sheikhs like a hen around her chick. Afterwards I met him in the bar, and steered the conversation round to the question of slavery. He indignantly denied that there were any slaves in Oman, and proceeded to read me a long lecture about "half-baked journalists and left-wing M.P.'s who didn't know what they were talking about." When I mentioned Raymond O'Shea's book *The Sand Kings of Oman*, in which he deals very fully with the question of slavery in Oman, he declared that he had never heard of the bloody fellow. When I mentioned Dr. Paul Harrison he finished his drink and walked out to join his Sheikh.

Chapter V

ZANZIBAR

MY CONTACT WITH the slave trade in Zanzibar came about in the most extraordinary way. Everybody knows that once Zanzibar was the clearing house for slaves; the unfortunate people bought or stolen in Africa were driven in herds along the old slave roads to the coast and then taken to Zanzibar, there to await auction and eventual shipment to Arabia. The auction block where many thousands of them stood, naked, the better to display their potentialities, still stands in a local church there.

I had flown down from Nairobi to see this once famous centre of slavery. I wanted to see the rich white houses with their beautiful brass-studded doors where the slave merchant princes once lived, the courtyards where their slaves were herded like cattle, the swift sailing dhows that once transported them, packed like sardines, to Arabia, and which now transport cloves and spices, the main exports of the island. Slavery was past history, a dark chapter in this beautiful island's story. That is what I thought but I was quickly disillusioned.

As I entered the bar of the Zanzibar Hotel on the evening of my arrival I heard a man saying in a very drunken voice "I am a descendant of the last king of Ireland, I am a descendant of the last king of Ireland." It went on and on, like a record when the needle gets caught in a groove. The man, a well-built Irishman of about fifty, was swaying over the bar, a whisky glass clutched in his hand. Nobody seemed to be taking any notice of him. Occasionally he buttonholed the barman, a native, and peering at him bleary-eyed, demanded "Am I the descendant of the ancient kings of Ireland or am I not, you black bastard?" "Yes, Mr. K. sir, of course you are," the bartender said. "Of course I am, and what's more I can prove it." Suddenly he noticed me, a stranger, and lurched towards me drunkenly, "Am I not the descendant of the ancient kings of Ireland?" he demanded truculently. Of course I should have laughed, treated it as a joke, but I was suffering from a hangover as a result of the send-off party in Nairobi the previous night, and the long tiring plane flight had not improved my temper. "To hell with the ancient kings of Ireland," I said. He stopped as if I had pole-axed him. "Who the hell are you?" he demanded. "John is my name," I said, "we are descended from the ancient kings of Munster who could lick the pants off the ancient kings of Ireland any day."

Fortunately he had a sense of humour. He extended a huge paw and said "Welcome to Zanzibar, John. Have a drink." Ignoring my protests he ordered two double whiskies. "Now we will consider your statement like the wise rational men we are. I presume you are referring to O'Ceallacain Cashel who defeated King Brian Boru before he became king of all Ireland . . ." Soon we were deep in Irish history. This was my first introduction to Pat K, one of the most charming and delightful men it has been my pleasure to meet.

Pat, although he did not tell me so himself, was head of the island's C.I.D., and had had an extraordinary career. A large landowner in Wicklow, Ireland, where he still held lands, he fought through the second World War, seeing action on most fronts; became bodyguard to King Farouk; a Palestine police officer; a Kenya police officer; and finally ended up as head of Zanzibar's C.I.D. Although he drank heavily there wasn't an ounce of harm in him. He was loved by everybody, except perhaps the proprietor of the Zanzibar Hotel, whom he regarded as "a snobby old bitch," although Pat was as great a snob as anybody. He loved his "coons" as he called the natives, and woe betide anyone who said anything against them. They, for their part, regarded him much as an Irish peasant regarded the squire of the old days, with respect for the institution he represented, coupled with an affection for the man himself.

He hated one man, and as he said himself, he hated him "like the devil hates holy water," and later that evening I was to see an example of the ferocious hatred with which he regarded him, and which he had to restrain because of his official position.

It came about in this way. In the lounge of the hotel were two American girls whom I had seen in the lounge of the New Stanley Hotel in Nairobi. They had just returned from a safari, and had flown to Zanzibar in the same plane that I had. Now they were obviously being pestered by a half-caste who seemed to be inviting them to go somewhere. I drew K's attention to the scene. "That dirty little pimp" he said, "O God," it was almost a prayer, "give me one chance to get him, just one chance, that is all I ask of You." "Who is he?" I asked, "He's the greatest, dirtiest little procurer this side of Arabia" he ground out savagely, "we've been watching him for years. We know he's in the slave traffic, but we can't prove it. He has never slipped up, never put a foot wrong. His Arab whore of a mother should have drowned the bastard at birth, and I mean bastard literally, for his father was a former governor of Zanzibar." "You have no proof of his connection with the slave trade?" "That's the damnable part of it, all we have are rumours, conjectures, suspicions. He has no visible means of support, since his father died, yet he lives better than I do. He is hand in glove with every rogue and vagabond in Zanzibar. Although he doesn't have to do it as there is no colour bar in Zanzibar, he spends most of his time drinking with dhow captains in the native bars. Every couple of years he does a grand tour of Europe, London, Paris, Rome, Hamburg, the lot. How does he manage all this without an income? I suggest we ask the girls to join our company." I went over to them. As I approached the half-caste left, scowling at me. I introduced myself and asked them to join us. They seemed delighted to be rescued from the half-caste. "What a horrible man" one of them exclaimed. "He was most pressing in his invitation to us to see the island by moonlight." "Pretty lucky you didn't go" Pat said, "the last

American girl who accepted his invitation was later found by two of my men in a native beer house. She was dancing on a table, nearly naked, and obviously drugged or very drunk. She was lucky my men found her when they did."

We spent a very pleasant evening talking and drinking. Pat had all the Irish blarney, and could be very charming, especially where ladies were concerned. He seemed to reach a certain stage of drunkenness quickly, and never progress beyond that point, no matter how much more he drank.

Next evening the four of us met again. Pat was in his usual good form. We were sitting in the bar when the half-caste came in, obviously very drunk. "Good evening Mr. K." he said as he passed us. "Don't speak to me," Pat growled. "All right, K," the half-caste said. "But remember one thing, this is an Arab country, our country. Soon you will be out of it altogether." "I told you I had nothing to say to you," Pat said.

"Look at the big police chief," the half-caste jeered, "the big Irish police chief. For years he has been trying to trap me, he and his stool pigeons, and hasn't been able."

I thought Pat would explode. Only the presence of the American girls restrained him. He went outside and returned with one of his inspectors, an Indian. "Remove that thing," he said, "and if he gives the slightest trouble shove him in the clink for the night. I don't care what influence he has on the island." It was the first hint Pat had given that everything wasn't what it seemed with his job. The incident seemed to have spoiled the party, and we broke up soon after.

Next day my taxi-man, who had witnessed the scene in the bar said, "That is a dirty piece of work. Sooner or later he will provoke Mr. K into striking him, which is what he wants. Then he can scream to all the Arabs that he was assaulted by a white policeman, which in an Arab state could cause a lot of trouble. Nobody likes him, but he has a lot of influence in high quarters." "Because he is a slaver?" I shot at him. He looked at me in amazement. "How did you know that?" he asked. "I get around and hear things," I answered. "Is it true?" "Nobody knows for certain," he answered slowly, "there are many rumours. Occasionally a girl disappears from the island, nobody knows where she gets to. Last year two young Indian girls were missing and were never found. Sometimes strange dhows put in here from other places, with girls, sometimes white girls, aboard. Nobody is allowed near them. The captains always call on the half-caste. It is all very strange." Strange indeed. Once Zanzibar was the centre of the trade in black ivory, as the slave trade was called. Is it now the centre of "white ivory," a clearing centre for white girls who have been abducted and sent there?

Chapter VI

THE BELGIAN CONGO

ALTHOUGH HUNDREDS OF human beings are taken each year from the Belgian Congo to be sold in the slave markets of the Yemen and Saudi Arabia, true slavery, that is the ownership of one human being by another who holds power of life or death in his hands, does not exist there. How, then, are these people obtained? To answer that question it is necessary to go back a long way to the Berlin Conference of 1884-5. At that conference fourteen of the major European powers agreed to the International African Association which was formed by King Leopold of the Belgians, taking over an area of 900,000 square miles in the centre of Africa on the Congo river. This was to be known as the Congo Free State, a name which was later changed to the Belgian Congo. At this conference the new state was placed under the sovereignty of King Leopold in his personal capacity. Its aims were twofold; the suppression of the slave trade, which was then at its peak under Arab slavers, and the moral and material well-being of the natives in the territory.

Stanley became an agent for King Leopold when the new State was formed. He defined his duties as an agent in the following words: "The novel mission of sowing along its banks civilised settlement, to peacefully conquer and subdue it, to remould it in harmony with modern ideas into National States, within whose limits the European merchant shall go hand in hand with the dark African trader, and justice, law and order shall prevail and murder and lawlessness shall for ever cease." Alas for the idealism of Stanley and the King. In a few short years the name of the Congo became a by-word throughout the civilised world for cruelties perpetrated on the natives there far in excess of anything carried out in the slave-owning countries.

Because of the climate the "European merchants" did not flock to the Congo as Stanley had expected. Instead it became the Mecca for the penniless adventurer, the shady and the greedy. Rubber could be had there in plenty, and at that time there was a world-wide demand for rubber, due to the invention of the rubber tyre, bringing untold wealth to the Europeans. The "black African trader" with whom Stanley had hoped the European trader would go "hand-in-hand" found he had no part in his country's economy. In 1890 it was decreed by the Belgian Government that the products of the forest was their property, that the natives owned nothing but their villages and gardens. But rubber had to be collected, and this could not be done by the white man. Accordingly, the natives were pressed into service. A system was set up which made the system of indentured labour in South Africa today sound like a Sunday school picnic. The country was divided up into areas, with a white official in charge of each area. He was directly responsible for the collection of the rubber, and as he was paid on a percentage basis it was naturally in his own interest to see that the greatest possible amount was collected. Under him, he had a corps of native guards, quartered in the villages, under the command of the native overseer. Their job was to see that natives, young or old, went to the forest and collected the rubber, ten pounds each week. Their women and children were held as hostages to guarantee their return. If a man returned without his quota of rubber he was mercilessly flogged. If he returned a second time without his tally not only was he flogged, but his women and children were flogged before his eyes. If all the men of the village returned without the full quota of rubber the village was burned down. For this labour each man was paid the magnificent sum of six shillings and four pence per year. Hundreds of thousands of men died in the forests or through the brutality of the native overseers. These were drawn from the very scum of the population and, according to a report published later, "abused their authority, became despots demanding women and victuals, not only for themselves but for vagabond parasites whom the love of rapine attaches to them like a regular body-guard. They kill without pity all who offer resistance to their demands or caprices." The black soldiers were ordered to bring back from the forest human hands which were checked against the number of cartridges fired. Although the population dwindled the amount of rubber to be collected by each village remained fixed, and new atrocities were resorted to in an endeavour to force the natives to return their tally. If they failed, their women and children were crucified. Men who did not return with their tally were beheaded and their sexual organs hung on posts around the village. It is estimated that in thirty years, the total population of the Belgian Congo dropped from 30,000,000 to 8,000,000 people.

At length, reports began to reach the outside world of the atrocities perpetrated in the Belgian Congo, sent by missionaries who worked there. These reports were strenuously denied by the King and the Belgian authorities. Indeed, one member of the Belgian Parliament, Carton de Wiart, described them as the "vapourings of worthy souls whose reserves of sentimentality are often injudiciously employed." In these denials the King and Government were supported by the Belgian newspapers. However, the reports became so numerous and well-documented that they could no longer be ignored. The Catholic Church took a hand, and the Jesuits were ordered to give up tracts of land granted to them by the Administration.

Public opinion, particularly in Britain and America, two of the foremost signatories to the Berlin Act of 1885, was aroused. Article six of this Act read: "All powers exercising rights of sovereignty or influence in the said territories engage themselves to watch over the conservation of the indigenous populations and the amelioration of their moral and material conditions of existence and to strive for the suppression of slavery and especially of the Negro slave trade."

King Leopold was forced in 1904 to send an International Commission, consisting of three judges, a Swiss, a Belgian and an Italian, to the Congo to study conditions there. When they returned he refused to allow their findings to be published. He had good reason to do so; it transpired later that the King and his associates had made three million pounds profit in the first ten years of the take-over there. At length public opinion prevailed and in 1908 the King was forced to relinquish his personal control of the Congo. It was then vested in the Belgian people and Parliament. A short time later the Congo was visited by Prince Albert, heir to the Belgian throne, and although his reports were never published, conditions for the natives were ameliorated. Changes came about slowly, and even in 1911, three years after the Belgian Government had assumed responsibility for the Congo, a Belgian, M. Vandervelde, reported that forced labour still existed in half the area.

With the passage of years another form of slavery came into being in the Belgian Congo, the system of debt-bondage. It is a form of slavery created by indebtedness. Very often a native has nothing to offer as a security for credit or to repay a debt, but himself. To obtain money or to liquidate a debt, he enters into an agreement with his creditor whereby he must work in exchange for maintenance until the debt is repaid. It is a pernicious system, as the value of the service rendered is not credited towards the liquidation of the debt. Thus a landlord or company can maintain a hold over a debtor, who remains a slave all his life, or until the unlikely event of his family paying the debt. The system of debt-bondage in the Belgian Congo has been described by Madame Jane Vialle: "In the Belgian Congo the custom of pledging oneself or a third person in payment of a debt is known as Kivi. A Kivi is an insolvent debtor who gives himself up to a member of another clan on condition that the latter pays his debt. The Kivi becomes a slave, subject, however, to the reservation that he cannot be sold without the members of his clan having been first invited to set their clansman free by re-imbursing his owner."

This leads directly to the sale of slaves that takes place in the Belgian Congo today. Kivis are bought by agents for the Arab slavers. In most cases their people are too poor to reimburse the agents, and the Kivi is told that he will be sold outside the Belgian Congo. Of course he is terrified at the thought of being dragged away from his homeland, never to see his family or friends again. The agents, who have no intention of selling him, or in fact no possibility of finding a buyer for him outside the Belgian Congo, then suggest a compromise. Under the agreement he made when first entering debt-bondage he is permitted to provide a substitute, provided that substitute is acceptable to the creditor. The agents now suggest that perhaps he would like to provide a daughter or a young female relative as substitute. As a very low value is set on females in Africa the debtor jumps at the opportunity. He is freed and a young healthy girl is handed over to the slaver's agents, at a fraction of the cost that they would have to pay in the clandestine market. A consignment is made up, and one night they are run across the Sudanese border, on their way to the port of Suakin and slavery. Thus the evils of Leopold's misguided colonisation in the Congo still bears fruit today.

Chapter VII

SLAVERY IN AFRICA SOUTH OF THE SAHARA

THAT SLAVERY IN Africa south of the Sahara exists cannot be denied, although it is a different form of slavery from that operating in the Moslem countries or in India. Here slavery is almost entirely connected with the land, the tilling of the soil, the hewing of wood and the drawing of water.

African negroes, except for the detribalised Africans living in the large cities of Nairobi, Salisbury, Johannesburg or Cape Town, are passionately attached to the soil. The tribe and the tribal land are the centres of their existence. But although the African male is attached to the soil, he does nothing to cultivate it. This is left to the women and children. They are beasts of burden, the motor power for all agricultural operations. Women in the African tribes are treated as little better than cattle; indeed in some tribes, like the Masii, the cattle are considered more valuable.

The wives are bought as young girls at a very tender age, usually on reaching puberty. They have absolutely no say in the matter. The groom approaches his prospective father-in-law through an intermediary. There is a long palaver about the number of cattle or goats the bride is worth. Each side tries to beat down the other, like farmers bargaining over the price of a heifer at an English fair. The girl is brought out naked, and paraded before the assembled crowd to watch the fun. She is handled, pawed, and examined by the interested parties. Needless to say, she has no voice in the matter. She has never seen her prospective bridegroom before. Usually he is an old man, particularly if she is good looking, as a young man would not be able to afford the "bride-price" or lobolo. This is usually paid in cows or sheep. When the deal is completed she packs her grass mat and cooking pot, and accompanies her husband to his hut. Here, before she is allowed to enter, she must undergo her initiation. The husband already has five or six wives. They seize her, tie her up and she is soundly whipped by the senior wife. This is to teach her obedience. Her hymen is then broken by the most junior wife, and with memories of her own initiation fresh in her mind, is none too gentle with the newcomer.

After the initiation she is allowed into the hut, and becomes her husband's property, body and soul. Her life is that of a drudge to the other wives, and will remain so until her husband takes another wife. There is no sentiment in an African "marriage"; it is entirely a business deal. The husband owns everything, even her children. If she has a child by another man, and if the husband is old or impotent she is encouraged to do so, that child is also the property of the husband. I have seen old men in Kenya and Tanganyika shuffling along the trail, accompanied by five or six girls, the youngest probably no more than twelve or thirteen years old.

It was thought that when some of the Africans became de-tribalised this practice would cease, and that they would adopt the white man's ways when they moved to the cities. Instead the position became worse. They got jobs as taxi drivers, or in garages or as house-boys, and probably for the first time owned some money. Saving this, the African went back to his tribe, and with it bought a wife. He brought her to the city, installed her in a shack, and rented her out to his friends, who could not afford a wife. Soon he had the money to buy another wife which he duly did. He rented her out, and bought a third. In the course of a few years he had acquired nine or ten wives, all of whom were earning him a steady income. I know several taxi drivers in Nairobi, who have several wives acquired in this way. They say proudly that there is now no need for them to work but the taxis are useful for ferrying clients from the centre of Nairobi to the brothel districts of Eastleigh.

A surprising number of prominent Europeans patronise the girls there, men whose appetites for the dried-up European women have gone, and who demand something new in the way of a young virile thirteen-year-old girl from the tribes. If a child is born of the chance encounter between the white man and a native girl, the husband is delighted, particularly if she is a girl with light coloured skin. She is worth a lot of cows in the location.

British soldiers stationed in Kenya, particularly the Cameronians, have hundreds of light-skinned offspring now running wild with the native children around the locations. Their mothers, young girls bought by de-tribalised Africans living in Nairobi, are sent out in the streets after dark to solicit the troops. On pay-day one sees the waste ground in front of the Nairobi Railway Station thronged with hundreds of them. A few speak one word of English—D. H. Lawrence's four letter word; others make their needs known by the simple expedient of lifting up their dresses. They wear absolutely nothing underneath.

If a man dies his brother or nearest male relative is entitled to claim all his goods, including his wives and children. He can keep them or re-sell them as he thinks fit. They have absolutely no say in the matter. World public opinion was outraged and horrified, when at the height of the Congo riots following independence, Africans claimed white women whom they said they had bought, producing receipts as evidence. To the African there was nothing strange about it. It was a simple transaction— he had paid his money and he wanted the goods.

It will take years of teaching to make the African realise that human beings cannot be bought like cattle, and the departure of the Europeans from the African continent will set the clock back a century.

Chapter VIII

SLAVERY IN INDIA

SLAVERY IN INDIA is almost entirely due to economic factors and is closely connected with the oldest profession in the world. In Bombay alone, it is estimated that there are six thousand prostitutes, but nobody knows the exact figures. In Grant Road and Faulkland Road in Bombay are the famous cages. These are wooden huts or shacks with bars in front, where three or four girls operate. They stand at the bars and shout enticements to passers-by to come in and avail themselves of their services. The room, if one can call it a room, is partitioned by a curtain, and the services are provided behind the curtain. The man goes up to the cage and pays his money before he is admitted; he then selects his girl, takes her behind the curtain and avails himself of the services she provides. The time is short, usually a couple of minutes and then he is out again. If in the meantime another customer comes for another girl he has to wait until the room is vacated by the first client. All these girls are slaves, slaves to pimps and procurers. They range in age from twelve to twenty-five; after twenty-five the women are thrown out of the cages and have to scratch a living the best way they can as street sweepers or in some other degrading employment.

Occasionally hints of this slavery reach the outside world. Recently a reporter in one of the Indian newspapers did a series on slavery and prostitution in India. The first report appeared, but no subsequent reports followed. It was probably too embarrassing to Mr. Nehru, and his Congress party was too busy attempting to eradicate "slavery" as they called it, in the Congo or in Kenya or in Rhodesia or South Africa.

More recently, however, some facts on prostitution and slavery came to light at a meeting organised by The Association of Moral and Social Hygiene in India. Mr. Shantilal Shah, State Labour Minister, said that strong executive action and powerful public opinion alone could help in the eradication of prostitution. He was speaking as the Chairman of the Symposium on the implementation of the suppression of The Immoral Traffic Acts. Mr. Shah expressed a view that it might later become necessary to shift the onus of proof on the accused to prove his or her innocence. He said that no law could operate unless there was co-operation from the public.

Mr. S. H. J. Kanga, Superintendent of Police, Crimes Branch, C.I.D. at Bombay said that the biggest difficulty in enforcing the provision of the suppression of an Immoral Traffic Act was a lack of respectable witnesses to prove the prosecution's cases in the Law Courts. He said that a number of state witnesses had turned brazenly hostile and had no regard to the truth. The result was an acquittal of the accused. It must be remembered that these men were not speaking of actual prostitutes, they were speaking mainly of procurers, and the owners of girls who are slaves. If their earnings are not handed over to the procurers, they are liable to meet with sudden death or disfigurement for life. Many of the girls are sold by their parents to the procurers because they cannot support them.

In India, families are very large and any girl taken off the parents' hands for fifty or a hundred rupees represents a fortune to the parents, and is one less mouth to feed. Mr. Kanga pressed for the heaviest punishment on proved offenders, especially men who had escaped so far under the suppression of a Moral Traffic Act, and urged the state governments to provide for the maintenance, education, training and care of the children of prostitutes.

Prostitution, while responsible for slavery in most districts in India, is not, however, the primary factor in some of the country districts. Here children, boys and girls, are sold to a land-owner who puts them to work at an early age on his land and provides them with the bare necessities of life. It is in his own interest to get as much work out of them as possible, and to pay as little as possible for their food; as a consequence the malnutrition of these slave children is appalling. One sees them with bloated bellies, thin spindly arms and legs, attempting to lift heavy loads at which a grown man would baulk. I have seen many of these children in the Southern States of India, particularly in Madras. My sister is a Mother Superior in charge of several convents in Southern India. These convents are there for the purpose of rescuing children either abandoned by their parents or about to be sold into slavery; for a few rupees it is possible to purchase children up to nine years of age. When taken into the convent they are a pitiful sight; they are fed and clothed and eventually are taught a trade, such as weaving, basket making or metal work, and are then placed in positions where they at least can earn their own living. It is only fair to say that the Indian Government give these convents and the nuns every encouragement, even making a grant towards the maintenance of these children. However, there are so many and the grant is so small, the equivalent of five shillings a week for each child, that very many children are still sold into slavery in India.

The lives the girls have to lead is slavery in its very worst form. They must make for their procurer a certain amount of money each week; if not they are severely flogged. That is why, when going down Grant Road, particularly for a European, it is never safe to go on foot because these girls will suddenly open the barred cages and drag him in, whether he likes it or not. Grant Road is a long road approximately half a mile in length, and at one end are the very cheap girls who go with men for a couple of annas, about ninepence. They are patronised by the street sweepers and the very low-caste Indians. As one progresses up the road the quality of the girls, if one may term it that, improves, so that at the top of Grant Road one would pay the equivalent of a pound, which is thirteen rupees, for a girl. Falkland Road on the other hand is used almost exclusively for brothels by the Anglo-Indians or Eurasians as they are called. These girls are slaves no less than their sisters on Grant Road but they live in better surroundings. Each house has about ten girls who sit in a common room and wait for their clients. The client is met at the door by the Madame, who owns these girls body and soul. She in turn is acting for a procurer who may own seven or eight of these houses. The Madame's word is law. The girls are given a little of their earnings each week to buy toilette requisites, but in the main they are kept within the four walls of the house. Some of the Eurasian girls are very beautiful. They may be the offspring of a white sailor and a girl in Grant Road; if so, the mother who bore the child gets absolutely nothing for her; she is reared by the slave owner until she is twelve or thirteen, and is old enough to enter the brothel. Indians particularly will pay a very high price for the services of such a girl. As the girls become older their value depreciates until finally they end up at the lower end of Falkland Road. They are in a slightly better position than their sisters on Grant Road for they need not accept street sweepers. Their services end when they are about twenty-seven or twenty-eight; after that they are usually shipped to another city where they enter the equivalent of a Grant Road.

I spoke to one of these girls whose name was Nora, in Falkland Road. She was a beautiful girl of about twenty-one with reddish hair, blue eyes and a completely white skin. She was the offspring of an Irishman and an Indian girl. She was bought from the mother when she was three years old and brought up with several other white-skinned girls in a procurer's house. She told me that she remained there until she was twelve; she was then taken to Calcutta and soon sold to a slaver; she did not know what he had paid for her, she was merely told that he was her father and that she must obey him in everything. A couple of nights after the sale a drunken sailor came to her room and had intercourse with her; this was her first experience of sex; she soon found that she was expected to work eight hours every day and being young and beautiful she was given what is termed there the evening shift, from six o'clock in the evening until two o'clock in the morning. After three years in Calcutta she was taken by her owner to Bombay and placed in a house in Falkland Road, where she now resides. She told me that while in Calcutta she was often beaten by her owner and the Madame of the house, but in Bombay she was lucky; the Madame of the house was very kind to her and often gave her small sums for powder and lipstick and whatever she wanted. In this house I visited at 392 Falkland Road there were fourteen girls; all or at least a majority could pass as white girls, although one looked like a typical Chinese, her father being Chinese, her mother Indian. She was always sought out by the Americans and enjoyed a certain popularity because of this.

Girls are not the only slaves in India. Off Grant Road there are also cages for boys who are used by homosexuals and are slaves in every sense of the word. They are bought when fairly young as the girls are and placed by the procurers in these houses when they are about ten. Their time in the houses however, is very much shorter than those of the girls, and at eighteen they are kicked out to starve or exist as best they can.

Of course Bombay is not the only state where prostitution and slavery exist in India. At the all-Indian conference of the Association of Moral and Social Hygiene in India, already referred to, Dr. Sushila Nayyar, President of the Association, moved a resolution urging the central and state governments to see that the suppression of Immoral Traffic in Women and Girls Act 1956 was implemented simultaneously in all the districts of States in the country. He said that owing to non-implementation of the Act throughout the States there had been a shifting of brothels and prostitutes to places where the Act was not in force. The Conference urged the amendment of the Act by:

(a)   declaring prostitution illegal in all its forms;
(b)   entitling the senior police officer to delegate his powers to subordinate police officers not below the rank of inspector and;

(c) holding all trials under the Act before a bench of magistrates, consisting of one stipendiary magistrate and two honorary magistrates, one of whom should be a lady and;

(d) making all offences under the Act not liable to bail and remanding the women and girls accused under the Act in the custody of a protector.

In Pakistan the position is no better. I quote from a paper, *The Star*, published in Karachi, the issue dated November the 10th, 1960. It is headed:

"Hyderabad, November 10th.

"Six persons, including a young woman, Mukhtar Begun, were arrested here by the police for allegedly kidnapping teenage girls from various parts of West Pakistan. The police also recovered a beautiful blue-eyed girl, Zanurrud, alias Nargis. It is reported that they kidnapped young girls from the up-country areas, and brought them down to Hyderabad and other cities of what was formerly Sind, where they were sold to brothel keepers or to wealthy landlords. Zanurrud was allegedly kidnapped from Peshawar and brought to Hyberabad where she was forced to lead an immoral life. On getting a tip-off the police raided the house where Zanurrud was kept and recovered the girl. Later the same day six persons were arrested in Pakistan."

The Pakistan Government, unlike the Indian Government, are doing everything possible to stamp out this trade, but their efforts will have to be redoubled, and they must obtain greater public support if there is to be any improvement.

PART III

THE HISTORY OF SLAVERY SINCE ITS ABOLITION

IN 1815 THE great powers of Europe strongly condemned the slave trade but were, in general, content to do no more than state their abhorrence of it. The reasons advanced for doing nothing were that the tropical plantations could not be maintained without slaves; the force of custom hallowed the trade; interference in the trade would raise questions of national integrity under national flags at sea; and finally, attacks on the slave trade might hamper normal and licit commerce.

A few nations, among them Great Britain and Denmark, had forbidden their sailors and ships to carry slaves but many others were reluctant to do so. In the previous year the French had absolutely refused to condemn the traffic but Napoleon, during his "Hundred Days" had forbidden it throughout the French dominions. When the Congress of Vienna was reconvened after Napoleon's defeat at the battle of Waterloo, Talleyrand, the French delegate, could hardly reverse the ruling of the man whom the monarchs of Europe, including Louis XVIII of France, had called the Anti-Christ. In spite of this the French refused to use their navy to prevent the traffic as did the Portuguese, the Spaniards and the Americans. All these nations had tropical or sub-tropical possessions where, at the time, it was considered that only negro slaves could work. It must also be remembered that in 1815 Great Britain had not emancipated the slaves in her colonial possessions; she had merely forbidden the traffic by her mercantile marine.

The anti-abolitionists of the United Kingdom argued, with some accuracy, that if the trade had been forbidden to British ships this was only to the advantage of the ships of other nations. Indeed one of the chief difficulties which faced the Navy, now relieved from the blockading of Napoleonic Europe and so enabled to attack ships carrying slaves, was that in 1815 no nations were prepared to allow vessels flying their flags to be searched by warships of another nation. The Spaniards, Portuguese and French could not envisage their tropical plantations being worked by anyone but slaves and thus, while ostensibly condemning the traffic, were prepared to allow its continuance. The Americans had recently fought the war of 1812-1814 against the British precisely over the rights of their merchant vessels to evade such a search. Again, whereas the attitude of the Northern states of the Union was liberal and abolitionist, more than one of the Southern states had initially refused to join the Union if the right to use slaves was forbidden by the constitution. The English Navy was bedevilled in its attempts to prevent the carriage of slaves by sea because of this intransigence on the part of the United States until after Lincoln's election to the presidency in 1860.

Another argument brought forward by the anti-abolitionists was that by making the carrying of slaves an offence the would-be abolishers were making the state of the slaves at sea even worse than it formerly had been. The attacks on the trade made the supply of slaves to the tropical plantations sparser, therefore the cost of slaves increased and if anything the profit of the slavers became higher than it had been before. This being so it paid the traders well even if only one ship in three reached the slave-importing harbours. However, it was obviously a matter of elementary trading acumen that each slaver should carry as many slaves as it could hold, with the result that unfortunate Africans who were abducted from the coasts of their Continent were literally packed like sardines in the holds of the slave ships. In the 1830s, three hundred and four slaves of a cargo of seven hundred and twelve died whilst in transit, and these figures are by no means typical of the mortality rate of slaves at sea. It was said that slaves who had been freed after some time in the slavers were never again able to stand up straight. Naturally, disease among the slaves at sea was rampant, particularly smallpox, dysentery, and diseases of the eyes. One gruesome incident occurred in 1819. A slaver had picked up several negroes in Bonny, one of the principal African states from which slaves were exported; after some days at sea the crew of the ship became infected with ophthalmia, a very common disease among slaves in transit; so virulent was this epidemic that no man on board was able to navigate. The ship sailed blindly for ten days until with relief its crew heard the sound of another ship sailing close to them. They approached the ship guided only by their ears and saluted it. The master of the ship they had fallen in with called out that he could let them have provisions in plenty in return for hands; his crew also had been inflicted with ophthalmia.

The officers and men of the naval vessels concerned with preventing the trade also suffered seriously from diseases particularly those carried by mosquitoes. Not until towards the end of the nineteenth century was it realised that yellow fever and malaria were contracted as the result of mosquito bites, though a certain Surgeon Mckinnel aboard H.M.S. *Sybille* in 1830 employed a repulsive experiment to show that Yellow Fever was not contagious. He toasted the officers of his ship with a glass of black vomit taken from one of the men suffering from the fever and drank the glass dry. Everyone aboard expected him to die but he duly took his dinner with the rest a few hours later, his health unimpaired.

Although after 1815 British warships patrolled the seas capturing slaving vessels and freeing the slaves, it was another eighteen years before slaves throughout the British Empire were emancipated. There still remained many unfortunate men and women in this state of bondage; it was estimated in 1841 that there were six and a half million slaves under Christian governments. An example of the size of the trade is given by the fact that in the 1830s more than one hundred thousand slaves were imported into Brazil alone, in eighteen months. It was then, as it still is today, difficult to obtain figures of the number of slaves carried but a modest and probably accurate assessment was that after

1825, until about 1840, the average number of slaves annually exported from Africa was one hundred thousand and that about three thousand were annually freed.

In 1841 the situation became somewhat better; a conference on the slave trade was held in London and several great powers including Britain, Austria and Prussia agreed that all ships carrying slaves should be treated as pirate ships. This gave the Navies of the powers concerned the right of search of vessels of all the nations which had signed the treaty. But there was a saving clause that this treaty was not to be effective in the Mediterranean and Red Seas, two of the areas where the trade was heaviest for the markets of the Arab powers. Spain, Portugal and the United States did not sign this treaty and France, although agreeing to it, did not ratify it in her legislature. And although Spain had agreed, in a treaty of 1835, to allow British warships the right to search her vessels and apprehend them regardless of whether or not there were slaves aboard, so long as the ships carried the implements of the trade, she did nothing herself to prevent it. The question of rights of search and of evidence were somewhat clarified by the conference of 1841. Until that date, apart from the case of Spanish ships, which has just been described, British naval vessels were unable to take ships regardless of the evidence that they were slavers, unless the ships were actually carrying slaves. This having been so, when a suspicious ship was approached at sea by a man-of-war she could either hoist the colours of a foreign nation or, if she were fast enough, could land her slaves on the coast and wait for the patrol vessel to go away. Even after 1841 it was still possible for slavers to hoist either French or American colours or again to go to a harbour where she could temporarily jettison her cargo.

Both Spain and Portugal had been paid large sums by Britain for the losses of revenue they would sustain when they gave up the trade, as they had agreed to do by treaty, but, in spite of this, they continued to allow their vessels to maintain it. The case of the United States was similar. Although slavery, as such, was still legal there and was, of course, an extremely common practice in the Southern states, she had formally abolished the *trade* as early as 1807, but her Presidents and the leaders of her Navy did very little to prevent it—except for one or two periods during the 1840s when English and American patrols worked together. Apart from the difficulties of search of slavers flying the American flag, it must also be considered that the ports and anchorages afforded to these ships off the coast of Florida were very difficult to patrol. There were many points at which vessels could sail inland up scarcely mapped rivers and there were many parts of the Everglades region where the passages were so tortuous and intricate that naval ships could hardly hope to follow, trace, or keep watch on the numerous slave ships which used the area as a point from which slaves could be landed and transported to the cotton plantations of the "Deep South."

All this being so, the United States merchant marine became the foremost in the slave trade and, there being a premium on speed and space aboard vessels—to avoid capture and to carry as many slaves as possible—the American ship-building industry benefited greatly from the advances made in the design of fast ships with large holds. An incident which might be considered amusing were it not concerned with the sale of human beings as stock illustrates this point. The United States Yacht *Wanderer*, a vessel owned by a rich member of the New York Yacht Club, was sold to one Captain Corrie, who acquired a wealthy patron and set off for the coast of the Congo, ostensibly on a cruising holiday. Near the coast he met the British patrol vessel, H.M.S. *Medusa*. He challenged this ship to a race; the challenge was accepted and the American duly won. After the race was over Captain Corrie entertained the captain and officers of the *Medusa* to dinner and jokingly suggested that his ship, the *Wanderer*, would make an excellent slaver as she could beat the fastest opponent the British could put against her. He then went on to ask his guests if they would care to inspect his hold to see if he had any equipment for transporting slaves aboard. If the British officers had accepted his invitation they would have been surprised to discover that this supposed pleasure cruiser was indeed fitted up as a slaver. Having discovered that the British ship had no chance of catching the *Wanderer*, her captain sailed into the Congo and picked up a cargo of young slaves. He then set sail back to America. On reaching the mouth of the Savannah river he again needed bluff for there was a fortress at the mouth of the river to prevent slavers sailing up it and landing their cargoes. So he invited all the officers of the fortress to a military ball and while the festivities were proceeding the *Wanderer* quietly slipped up the river. The story of these two cases of legerdemain soon got abroad and as a result Captain Corrie was expelled from the New York Yacht Club, but suffered no other penalty.

The marine architects of the United States, however, were not the only ones to benefit from the advances in the design of vessels; one of the reasons for the introduction of screw-steamers into the British Navy was that if the Navy were to be successful in the prevention of slave trading it needed the fastest ships on the seas—screw steamers were, of course, swifter than any other vessels. In addition to the gain made in the design of British warships indirectly due to the need to counter the slavers—there were other inducements to modernise the Navy—Great Britain incidentally gained many colonial possessions in this way.

Before the "Scramble for Africa" late in the nineteenth century, there was little desire in England for more colonial territories—although politicians of other countries alleged that the British reasons for attacking the slave trade so vigorously were hypocritical and designed only to further legitimate British trade and the acquisition of territory abroad. In spite of the abolitionists' arguments that the best way to prevent the trade was by taking the ports and coastal areas from which it was carried on, the Manchester school of Cobden and Bright, for once supported by other parliamentarians, such as Disraeli, urged that Britain should not attempt to acquire more territories, whatever the reasons for so doing, but should rather make treaties with the rulers of the African states from which slaves were exported. Several treaties by which these rulers agreed to refrain from the trade were, in fact, made but they were rarely honoured and in more than one case the British found it necessary to overthrow the native kings and take possession of their lands. The acquisition of Lagos is perhaps the most famous example of such action.

The area of Dahomey around the lagoon of Lagos was one of the principal African territories from which slaves were shipped across the Atlantic. When the first British embassies visited the area in 1845 they found a kingdom in which skulls were used for architectural ornament, a kingdom whose best soldiers were Amazons, troops of women soldiers whose chief occupation was to make armed raids on the surrounding countryside to capture as many of the natives thereof as they could lay hands on, for the purpose of enslaving them and selling them to the traders. A horrific type of sport was the chief entertainment provided by the king for the populace of Dahomey—it consisted of hurling live human beings from the walls of the palace into a pit twenty feet below. Those of the victims who were not killed by the fall were then set upon and murdered by the watching crowds and their bodies thrown to the vultures. For fifteen years the British negotiated with the rulers of this barbarous, if picturesque area but with little success. Finally, in 1861 the kingdom was annexed by Great Britain.

It should be noted that the trade carried on from African chiefdoms, such as Dahomey, was principally for the plantations of Brazil and Cuba, and also, of course, for the "Deep South" of the United States. The two branches of the trade, to Brazil and to Cuba, were, in the abolitionists' point of view, in a sense, complementary in that as one declined the other seemed to expand, and vice versa. In 1846, when Britain became a free trade nation and among other measures abolished the duties on Cuban sugar, the abolitionists predicted that as a result there would be an increase in the trade in slaves to that Spanish colony. Initially their prophecies were belied, chiefly because for a period of about seven years the colonial governors, abiding by the agreements made between Britain and Spain, prevented the trade. However, around the year 1846 the trade between the African states and Brazil flourished. Although the independent state of Brazil had formally abolished the trade in 1826, little had been done by the Brazilians to prevent its continuation. Primarily, it has been argued, this was so because, in spite of the good intentions of the legislature of that country, the power in the state lay, as ever, where the massed capital lay, and the capitalists of this former Portuguese colony were the plantation owners and their allied slave traders. Palmerston, that beau ideal of the worshippers of British might, was little impressed by lesser breeds without the law or by territorial rights and he countenanced—if that is not too weak a word—anti-slaving operations by British warships in Brazilian territorial waters. As a result the Brazilians were formidably impressed with the British powers of coercion and in the early eighteen fifties the trade to Brazil was virtually at an end. However, even after the trade had ended a British warship discovered a vessel which seemed to be bound for Brazil; it appeared to be owned by Portuguese traders; its crew comprised a cross section of rogues of all nations and as for its papers, these had been thrown overboard when the British ship had been sighted and the captain claimed that he was a citizen of the Papal States.

As has already been mentioned, the trade with Cuba declined as it increased with Brazil; after the Brazilian trade had been virtually ended that between Africa and Cuba once again began to flourish. There were several reasons for this: firstly the outbreak of the Crimean War in 1854 withdrew many of the British ships engaged on the prevention of the traffic from the Atlantic; secondly, the Spanish colonial governors who had previously been unfavourable to the trade were now replaced by others who were less scrupulous; finally, the plantations and trading affairs of Cuba were largely backed by American capital; the slave ships of Cuba were owned by citizens of the United States and the finance behind the trade was American. As has already been mentioned, the United States' leaders were understandably very loth to allow any other nation to search United States' ships at sea and this too added to the difficulties of the patrollers. Nor were the Americans alone in refusing search rights; the French too were concerned at what they considered an infringement of national sovereignty, and their ships carried slaves when the Americans' did not.

Lincoln's election and the outbreak of the American Civil War put an end to this intransigence. In 1862 a treaty was signed between the United States and Britain whereby the Navies of each nation were given mutual rights of search of each other's vessels. From this time onwards the trade to Cuba began to decline and a sign that nations with less advanced and libertarian views were coming round was given in 1865 when for the first time the Spaniards executed a slave trader.

Although by the mid-eighteen seventies the Atlantic trade was as good as ever the traffic in slaves had not been entirely eradicated—as it has not been to this day. The most important scene of the trade after the Atlantic was in the area of the Indian Ocean and the Arabian Sea off the Gulf of Persia. From this area the trade into the Arabian states still continued. And it was an area in which the British navy was less successful than it had been in the Atlantic. Once again there was the difficulty of vested interests. The French, who had formally forbidden slavery throughout their dominions, at best turned a blind eye to, at worst connived in, the carrying of indentured labour, *emigrés libres*, to their tropical possessions. This labour which was, in effect, slave labour—an interpreter, speaking French, Arabic and African tongues would inquire of the natives if they were willing to work at such and such terms in the French possessions (not that the terms ostensibly agreed to were frequently observed) and would then inform the officers of the vessels awaiting their cargo that the natives had so agreed—this labour force was imported from the Arabs who traded in slaves off the coast of north-east Africa.

Another difficulty, from the point of view of the captains of British warships, was that the abolition of slavery had become in itself a vested interest. That is to say that the Admiralty had modified the methods by which warships were supposed to approach slavers, search them and carry off their cargoes. Unfortunately the Admiralty seemed to have learnt too much of the method of operations in the Atlantic because it rigorously laid down the way in which these should be followed, and these methods were completely useless on this other side of Africa. Here the trade was carried on by dhows, small, light coastal traders of shallow draught which the clumsy warships could not approach except in deep water and where the speed of the dhows made it difficult for the ships' boats to overtake and apprehend them.

At about this time too there was a recurrence of slavery in British possessions, which gave the critics of Britain genuine cause for complaint that she was not practising what she preached. Throughout the nineteenth century Australia had been in the process of development and in Queensland there were sugar plantations which required labour which was unsuitable for Europeans and, it evidently seemed to the plantation owners to be suitable for slave labourers used to a tropical climate. Thus a profitable trade, known as "Blackbirding" had grown up between Queensland and the Polynesian islands. Once again there was difficulty over national integrity; some of the islands were British and some were French and although joint courts were set up to judge traders it was alleged that the French courts were notoriously more lenient than the British ones.

An explosion of enraged public opinion in Great Britain was caused in the eighteen seventies by an incident which occurred in connection with the trade in this area. Bishop Patteson was a missionary who was very popular among the Polynesian islanders. Some "Blackbirders" disguised their ship to resemble the Bishop's *Southern Cross* and went round the islands asking the natives aboard "to see the bishop." Duly impressed, the natives went aboard and the traders carried them off into slavery. Some time later the bishop visited one of the islands which had been previously called upon by the bogus *Southern Cross* whereat the outraged natives murdered him.

The importation of Kanaka labour into Queensland continued until 1898 in spite of laws prohibiting it being passed both in Australia and Great Britain. Even when, in 1878, abundant Chinese labour became available in the territory the local government imposed heavy taxes on the Chinese preferring the cheaper working costs of the Polynesians to the labour of free Chinese. The only reason why the use of Kanaka labour was finally abandoned was because the islands from which these men were taken had been almost depopulated. It is only fair to say that after the "Bishop Patteson incident" the working conditions of the Kanakas in Queensland were considerably improved.

It was not until about ten years before the opening of the twentieth century that what may be called the classical slave trade began to be thoroughly opposed by the European nations. In 1885 a congress was held at Berlin to consider the Congo, which King Leopold II of the Belgians had recently commissioned Stanley, famous for his encounter with Livingstone, to explore. At the time the Congo basin was an area from which the Arab slave traders still made their depredations on human livestock: the members of the congress recognized in principle that the best means of preventing the trade was that the lands from which it was carried on should be held by an abolitionist power; they declared that the members of the Congress wished to protect the natives: to forbid slavery: to establish freedom of trade: to further missionary endeavours and exploration of the huge area. The aims of this conference appeared to be substantiated in 1889 and 1890 by the conferences at Brussels. The first conference assigned to Belgium, or rather to the Belgian king, the territories to be known initially as the "Free Congo" and later as the Belgian Congo. The second conference, that of 1890, resulted in what has been called the "Slaves' Magna Carta" being signed by almost all the civilised states of the world. The convention to which these nations agreed was by far the most effective weapon against slavery that has ever been made. By it the signatory powers agreed to do all they could to suppress slavery: there were sections of it dealing with the capture of slave ships at sea; the establishment of order in Africa, to prevent the trade from continuing there; the signatories were obliged to make severe laws against slavers of their nationality; and an international bureau to co-ordinate and effect the measures taken, was set up at Brussels. Additionally the nations, such as the Ottoman Empire and Persia, which still recognised domestic slavery agreed to aid in the prevention of the traffic in slaves.

The period following the ratification of the convention—in 1892—until the First World War was the heyday of the abolitionists but one aspect of the two congresses might be considered to have done more harm than good: the recognition of Belgian territorial rights in the Congo.

This enormous area had been assigned to King Leopold almost as a private estate, and a very rich private estate it was too. At first the prime raw material which was produced there was rubber, and the conditions under which this crop was gathered by the natives of the Congo were indistinguishable from slavery. Rubber was at the time very costly, and under King Leopold all distribution, control and marketing of it belonged to the state. The system by which it was gathered was that two thousand white agents, who controlled levies of soldiers, enforced its collection by the natives. The agents and their soldiery billeted themselves on the Congolese villages and while the native men were forced to go further and further afield, as the nearby wild crops were exhausted, the native women had to feed their masters. The harder the natives were worked the larger were the profits of the factors; for every kilo of rubber the agents could produce at five centimes or less they, the agents, gained a commission of fifteen centimes; for rubber produced at six or more centimes the agents could only obtain a commission of ten centimes for themselves. Thus it paid the agents of the king to drive the natives as hard as they could be driven and there was no power other than that of the king to investigate the methods by which the natives were induced to work. The agents with armed overseers drove the negroes so heartlessly that it was said that the Congo had been better before the Europeans arrived, in spite of the terror of the natives that they might at any time be carried off into bondage by Arab slavers. A Prime Minister of Belgium at the time remarked, "the native is entitled to nothing, what is given to him is a mere gratuity." More than one commission was sent to the

Congo to inquire into the labour system but little was done about it until the late nineteenth century, after Leopold was dead and the territory was being administered for the Belgian nation, rather than as the personal property of its monarch. Leopold had initiated his reign of the Congo as a liberator, he ended it as a speculator, concerned only with enriching himself, his country and his agents, regardless of the conditions under which his black subjects provided wealth for his white ones.

Not only in the Congo did increased demand for rubber lead to forced labour and conditions scarcely distinguishable from those of slavery. In Peru, another rubber-producing country, British financial interests were, in the early part of the twentieth century, connected with a large firm employing forced, or enslaved, labour. The Peruvian Amazonian Company, which had its headquarters in London, used as its labour force the Indians of the neighbourhood, the Putaymos. The system employed there differed slightly from that of the Belgians in the Congo. As payment for future work the Putaymos were advanced goods in return for which they provided labour. In fact, the terms were such that the Indians were unable to honour their obligations and many of them fell into a state known as "debt-bondage" in which state, because of their debts, they themselves became negotiable. In the same way as a farmer owing another money might cancel his debt by handing over cattle or produce, one agent could deal with another agent using Indians as a means of payment. Naturally, it was difficult to obtain information of the means of employment used in this remote part of the world and the company managed to prevaricate successfully for some time —on one occasion a member of the firm agreed to give a statement to a journalist; the journalist was handed an envelope in which he expected to find an account of what was going on in the plantations and discovered that instead he had been rewarded with a bank note of a large denomination. Eventually a law case was brought against the company and in 1913 it was dissolved.

Forced or indentured labour, often comparable to that used in the case of the Peruvian Amazonian Company, which has just been described, was often employed during the nineteenth century, particularly by European powers with tropical overseas possessions. France, with her system of *emigrés libres*, used forced labour as did Portugal, and still does so. Great Britain, the abolitionist power *par excellence*, also made use of this labour: after the slaves had been emancipated throughout British possessions coolie labourers from India were taken to the West Indies, where their status was very similar to that of slaves, and this continued for ten or twenty years after the Emancipation Act; today their descendants comprise a large proportion of the population of the West Indies.

It may be wondered what happened to the descendants of other slaves, those freed from the slave ships of the nineteenth century. Many of these men and women were resettled in two African states, one, American inspired and today independent, Liberia; the other a British colony, Sierra Leone.

Apart from a limited amount of smuggling into the Arabian peninsula, by the outbreak of the First World War the traffic in slaves had been virtually suppressed, although there was something of a recrudesence in the trade in parts of the Arab world during and after the war. However, slavery as an institution was still recognised and retained in several remote parts of the world. During the twenties and thirties of this century several of the countries in which slaves were still owned declared that slavery was about to be ended there or had been abolished. In some cases the abolition seems not to have been very thorough, for example, although Ethiopia, which had been conquered by the Italians in 1942, had from its Emperor, Haile Selassie, a declaration that slavery was to be abolished in that nation—in spite of this, eighteen years later, in 1955, there were still reports of slaves escaping from Ethiopia into parts of the Sudan. Also travellers in the Sahara Desert have given descriptions of the tribes of Tuaregs which still hold slaves. It has also been alleged that in certain South American states the condition of peonage, or serfdom, still exists.

Perhaps even the British Commonwealth has not been

thoroughly ridden of slavery; in the nineteen fifties there were prosecutions brought against slave-owners in Nigeria. Probably during the twentieth century the area of the British-dominated section of the world which still most flagrantly retained slavery has been Hong Kong. As in China proper, a traditional practice was the sale of children by poor parents. Sometimes this has been disguised as apprenticeship into domestic service. In Hong Kong today it seems almost certain that this so-called "Mui Tsai," has finally been eradicated. But it is believed that, at the date of writing, the government of India has not entirely done away with the practice of slavery in some of the extremely inaccessible areas of the nation.

PART IV

SLAVERY IN AFRICA AND ARABIA

HOUSE OF LORDS

Extracts from Parliamentary Debate
(Hansard)

Official Report Vol. 225 No. 104

Thursday 14 July 1960.

*Mr. Sean O'Callaghan and Anthony Blond Ltd.,
acknowledge with thanks the permission of
Her Majesty's Stationery Office
to reproduce the following debate.*

Slavery in Africa and Arabia

LORD SHACKLETON rose to ask her Majesty's Government what information they have on the continued existence of slavery, particularly in Africa and Arabia; what steps they propose to take to ensure the implementation of international conventions designed to bring this inhuman and degrading practice to an end, if necessary by the establishment of a special organisation within the United Nations, and whether they will raise this urgent problem at the July meeting of the Economic and Social Council of the United Nations. The noble Lord said: My Lords, we have just been discussing one of the new scourges of humanity, and I rise to ask the Question standing in my name in order to draw attention to one of the most ancient scourges that have afflicted mankind. It was only last year that the bicentenary of the birth of William Wilberforce was commemorated, and your Lordships are well aware that his Parliamentary life was mainly devoted to the abolition of slavery and that his work has been carried on by many able people since. It is now the general impression among people in this country that slavery no longer exists, and the object of my Question is not only to draw attention to the amount of slavery that there is in the world but to ask the Government what information they have from their sources upon this subject, and, in particular, to ask what steps they propose to take by way of international action or by other means to put an end to this degrading business.

There is no need, I think, to go into the history of slavery. I think it is universally accepted that, however well a slave may be treated, none the less it is in every way a repugnant basis of life for mankind. And of course European nations have no reason to be mealy-mouthed on this subject, or to be proud of the part they have played. We know that some of the great civilisations in classical times were built on slavery and that many European nations have played their part in the slave trade. But we do not need to waste time on the past. Our problem is to consider what there is in the way of slavery in the world today and what ought to be done to end it.

One of the difficulties is to get exact information, to collect from the the countries, where this slavery is practised, either openly or in a clandestine way, information on precisely what is going on. The chief centre of slavery in the world is still the Arabian Peninsula, and in particular Saudi Arabia, where it is estimated—and I must stress that it is only an estimate, and may be a very rough one—that there may be as many as half a million slaves today. My remarks will be mainly concerned with the slave trade as it relates to the Arabian Peninsula. It is the one region where the old chattel slavery still exists and is recognised as a legal status.

The countries of Arabia have theocratic government, and in them the law of the land is the *Koran*, which is supplemented by decrees made by the rulers. Slave owners and defenders of slavery —and this is important, because people are inclined to think that we should allow people to pursue their own historic customs— have argued that slavery is authorised by the *Koran* and by the teachings of the Prophet Mohammed, but the weight of evidence, I am told, is against this. Mohammed tolerated slavery in the backward community in which he lived, but at the same time he condemned it and intended that it should be progressively suppressed. Islamic writers of authority have stated in no uncertain terms that if the teachings of Mohammed on slavery had been applied in all Moslem countries, slavery would have ceased to exist, not only, as it has, in some of them, but in all. It is still practised not merely in Arabia but also the Yemen, Muscat, Oman and the small sheikhdoms and sultanates in the Aden

Protectorate. There is an abundance of evidence from unofficial sources, from travellers and residents in Saudi Arabia and those countries, that slavery exists there, and may, indeed, be increasing.

In 1936 the late King Ibn Saud of Saudi Arabia made a decree regulating the conditions of slaves. This decree largely restated the teachings of the *Koran*, requiring masters to be kind to their slaves. It also gave slaves certain rights to buy their freedom and, above all, it required slave owners to register their slaves with the Government. But while the principal aim was to help slaves throughout their servitude, as well as to provide some prospect of freedom, it also authorised, as I have said, the licensing of slave traders. That decree is still law, and there is plenty of evidence that the law is fully taken advantage of. This decree makes clear that it is part of the accepted pattern of life in those countries.

I should like to quote some of the further evidence that exists. Some of it is, I admit, old evidence, although collected in the last few years, and some of it may be already familiar to your Lordships. One of our difficulties, of course, is to get official, up-to-date information. There is evidence supplied not only by ministers. There was one which, I know, has already been quoted in this House. A French Protestant minister actually went to investigate rumours of slavery in French Africa and he reported in 1955 what he had found. In his report there is a dispatch written by the French Ambassador in Saudi Arabia. He stated that slave traders in Saudi Arabia were sending African emissaries to Africa to recruit slaves. They went and posed as Moslem missionaries and offered Africans a free pilgrimage to Mecca, which they said was being paid for by rich Moslems who had sinned and sought atonement in this way. Many Africans in the past few years have fallen into this trap. On arrival in Saudi Arabia they have been arrested for entering without a visa, and have been imprisoned and handed over to slave traders. The French Ambassador estimated the number who suffered that fate at a few hundred a year. The Government of Nigeria has since taken steps to try to limit this by licensing travel agencies, particularly those who deal with the Arabian countries.

There is, indeed, plenty of evidence, also coming from the same source, of African Moslems going on pilgrimages and taking several servants with them whom they sell on arrival, using them as living traveller's cheques. It is astonishing that faithful Moslems who believe in the teachings of their Prophet, can sit back and allow, if not connive at, the holy places of Islam being used to lure innocent Africans into slavery. There are numerous examples, too, some of them from official sources, of the actual practice of slavery in particular areas. We have known, for instance, of the name of the chief slave broker in Riyadh. His name was, at any rate a few years ago, Abdulla Ibn Marwan. We have the names of other slave dealers. There have been examples which have been brought from other countries of this practice. For instance, in Iraq, a certain slave dealer, Mohammad Husain, was captured and put on trial. He was found to have fifty kidnapped under-age girls ready to trans-ship to Riyadh. He was sentenced to ten years' imprisonment. In another place there have been examples of girls who have been kidnapped, and sometimes their relations have come out after them, trying to bring them back.

If anybody were to suggest that these slaves were always well treated, I would draw attention to a case, again well-founded, of twelve Baluchi slaves, some of whom were the personal property of the King of Saudi Arabia, who tried to escape. They were discovered, tracked down, and three were beheaded in the desert by the search party; others were brought back to Riyadh for public execution, where they were duly beheaded by a negro slave whose name was Al Hilali, in the square in front of the palace, to provide a lesson to other would-be escapees.

There are other travellers whose names will be known to your Lordships. Wilfrid Thesiger, whose book *Arabian Sands* has been so widely read, admittedly writing on a period about ten years ago, said:

"It seemed that the enormous wealth which was pouring into Saudi-Arabia from the American oil company had greatly increased both the demand for slaves and the price paid for them."

He had evidence because he met a caravan taking slaves actually along the road. James Morris, who was, I think, at one time a *Times* correspondent, is another well-known writer who has talked about slavery as a modern institution.

There are other areas in the world where slavery is practised. A Danish ethnologist has described the practice of slavery among the Tuaregs of the Sahara, and my noble friend Lord Maugham, who is shortly to speak, has some much more up-to-date and direct personal experience of this area. There is evidence collected by the Anti-Slavery Society through Commander Fox-Pitt, who went to West Africa and himself found plenty of evidence of this practice.

Finally, there has been some quite horrifying evidence of slavery in South America, in particular in Peru. It has been described in a book written by an American called Leonard Clark. If anyone should question it as a traveller's tale, I may say that a prominent Minister in Peru has written paying testimony to the reliability of the evidence, and promising that the Peruvian Government will take strong action

"to correct the shameful and inhuman slave practices which Clark found existed."

There has been slavery in China, although there is information that the new Chinese Government is taking strong steps to wipe it out. But, as I have said, one of our problems has been to get really up-to-date official information. There is a lot of evidence, but one needs much more precise evidence if action is to be taken.

I should like now to turn to the legal and international position with regard to slavery. The first really effective international action was taken in the Brussels Slavery Convention in 1890. This was effective because it had machinery written into it for supervising its application. It is possible that this Convention may still be in force, but it would probably be difficult to resuscitate because some of the signatories, like the Austro-Hungarian Empire, no longer exist. After the First World War the Slavery Convention of 1926 was signed under the auspices of the League of Nations.

This contained no machinery for supervision. It was not until after the efforts, largely of British initiative, of men like the noble Viscount, Lord Cecil of Chelwood, Charles Roden Buxton and others, that a special Committee was set up, which was successful to a considerable degree in not only collecting evidence but gradually reducing the slave traffic.

I emphasise the phrase "slave traffic." It is a question not only of the existence of slavery in countries where there are already slaves, but of a continuing traffic, going on from different parts of Africa. After the last war a new Convention was set up on the advice of a committee of experts. This was signed in 1956. It lacks any machinery for supervising its application. This is what I wish to draw to the attention of the Government, of the Minister and of the noble Marquess, who I am sure is well aware of this fact. Under the Convention reports are called for, but so far only one Government have supplied a report—that is, the British Government—and the Convention is in danger of becoming a dead letter.

It has been argued that it is the duty of the officials of the United Nations to take action to enforce Conventions, but in the opinion of many people that is not so. They are under no obligation to act unless they are directed to do so. What the Slavery Conventions need now is a Committee to examine information on slavery and to submit conclusions and recommendations to the Economic and Social Council. There are two possible forms of supervisory machinery. One is a special Committee, like the old Committee of the League of Nations. Another is to appoint a special consultant, a kind of Special Commissioner, who would collect information and advise the Economic and Social Council, which is, of course, the body responsible for the Slavery Conventions. The cost of this would be comparatively small.

My Lords, I should like to ask what Her Majesty's Government are going to do about this matter. In another place, in an earlier debate, the right honourable and learned gentleman the Foreign Secretary said (OFFICIAL REPORT, Commons, Vol. 590, col. 1313):

"I do not think the machinery is satisfactory."

This was said when he was questioned on the absence of permanent supervisory machinery: and I should like again to ask the question which was asked in another place: whether Her Majesty's Government are relying entirely on chance information and representations made by the Anti-Slavery Society. These reports come in and need to be investigated. Only in the last few days the Economic and Social Council have been meeting in Geneva, and I regret to say that it was left to representatives of voluntary bodies like the Society of Friends and the Anti-Slavery Society to raise the matter. I admit that some kind words were said by the British representative, but it was not on British initiative that any action was taken. The initiative came from the Danish delegate who moved a motion, on July 11, calling on all parties at least to supply the information they are supposed to supply under the Convention.

I feel it is particularly distressing that this country, which in the past has taken a lead in this matter, is failing to do anything very much about it at the moment. I would ask Her Majesty's Government to discuss this question and to make definite proposals, not only at the United Nations, but particularly among the new Commonwealth nations, because they will have a particularly important part to play. For as the white man withdraws from Africa—and this is true of French Africa, and, indeed, of Nigeria and Ghana—there is a risk that some of the slave trading that is going on will tend to increase. I am quite sure that the rulers of these new countries, the leaders in Nigeria and Ghana, would be perfectly willing to co-operate, and we (and when I say "we" I mean the world) need their co-operation if slavery is to be stamped out. Furthermore, there is a danger that if the British, and white men generally, press too hard on this matter they will be accused by the Russians and others of using it as an excuse for some colonialist policy. That is why I would urge Her Majesty's Government to make their approach on a very broad front.

It will be argued by some that slaves are better off than the free men of the country in which they live. And I do not for one moment deny that many slaves are exceedingly well treated and looked after, and are doing very well. This has always been part of the history of slavery. There have always been slaves who have risen to great positions, but the fact remains that this is not true of them all. Many of them find that they cannot get their freedom, and some of them are cruelly treated. The children of many of them are automatically born slaves, and young babies are still bought and sold as if they were cattle; and there is cruelty practised on some of them.

This is not one of the world's greatest problems, and just because it is no longer so it is in danger of falling out of the public eye. There is the possibility that slavery may linger on indefinitely. It is only through international action that it can be brought to an end, and I hope that we shall hear from Her Majesty's Government today, whatever are the difficulties in the way of preserving good relations with some of these smaller Arab rulers, that they will not shrink from expressing, in a very firm way, British opinion upon this. If they find it difficult to do much about it in territories where we exercise influence, I hope that at least they will speak out at the United Nations. It would be very sad if, for fear of offending some of the rulers of oil-bearing countries, we dared not take a lead in pressing for the freedom of the individual which this country has played so notable a part in doing in the past. I hope, therefore, that Her Majesty's Government will not trim their sails on this matter and that we shall get a forthright statement in reply to the Question I now ask.

5.43 p.m.

VISCOUNT MAUGHAM: My Lords, I must beg that indulgence which is bestowed by your Lordships on those addressing you for the first time. Recently I read an article which seemed to me relevant to the Question of my noble friend Lord Shackleton. It said:

"Among the calamities of war may be justly numbered the diminution of the love of truth, by the falsehoods which interest dictates, and credulity encourages. A peace will equally leave the warrior and relater of wars destitute of employment; and I know not whether more is to be dreaded from streets filled with soldiers accustomed to plunder, or from garrets filled with scribblers accustomed to lie."

The magazine was the *Idler*, dated November 11, 1758, and the author—as I expect your Lordships will have guessed—was Dr. Johnson. Times have changed since then, and I am glad to say that we no longer have anything to fear from the soldiers in our streets or, come to that, from the scribblers in our garrets. And I am all the more glad to say this because I was once a soldier and I am now most definitely a scribbler.

But the relevance of the quotation is this: in war and in cold war, truth is the first casualty, because both sides use propaganda. And propaganda is a boomerang which recoils upon the person who uses it. A Government puts out a distorted version of the truth and ends by accepting its own lies, and believing in them. The relevance of this to our present problem is this. Her Majesty's Government in general, and the Foreign Office in particular, have managed to convince themselves that slavery does not exist: and therefore, in the end, they have managed even to persuade the public that it is practically non-existent.

Why do the Foreign Office want to believe that slavery does not exist? Your Lordships have heard from the noble Lord, Lord Shackleton, that Saudi Arabia is the greatest slave-buying area in the world; and there are over half a million slaves there today. The main oil company operating in Saudi Arabia is the Arabian-American Oil Company—"Aramco"—and if it were known that children are enslaved in Saudi Arabia this might be taken as a criticism of Aramco's general moral influence over the country. Moreover, Aramco wields considerable influence in Washington; and the Foreign Office do not want to embarrass the Government of Britain's largest ally.

A friend of mine was attached to the Trucial Oman levies who in the autumn of 1955 captured the Buraimi Oasis from the Saudi Arabian forces. In one of the outlying villages in that uncertain frontier between Oman and Saudi Arabia, he discovered children in fetters. There they were, in a corner of the market place, and there were shackles on their ankles. This story haunted me, and so I approached the Anti-Slavery Society in London; I met more officers from the Trucial Oman levies; I consulted travellers; and all the sources confirmed what we have already been told, that Saudi Arabia is the main and largest market. And as the wealth has increased so, of course, the demand for slaves has risen, because a man is known by the number of slaves he has: it is a form of snobbery out there—like having a Cadillac. Whereas formerly an able-bodied man slave cost £50, he now costs £150. Whereas formerly an attractive girl cost £150, she now costs anything between £400 and £700.

There are two main slave routes into Saudi Arabia. The first comes from West Africa. It goes from the High Volta, through the Niger Provinces and the region of Timbuktu; across Africa to the Port of Suakin, and across the Red Sea, by dhow to Lith, a port south of Djedda. The other goes from Iraq and Persia, and Baluchistan across the Gulf and then, by caravans of camels, across to Riyadh. The children taken on this route are generally children bought from poor parents in these countries, but quite often they have been kidnapped. What happens to these slaves after they have reached the slave markets? Arabists have told us time and time again that, in fact, the lot of a slave is really not all that bad; that, after all, he is valuable property, and so it is worth while looking after him and feeding and clothing him. Certainly when I crossed the frontier into Saudi Arabia with Sir John Glubb in 1943 to visit the Emir Abdul Azziz el Sidar at Kaf, I saw no sign of ill-treatment of the slaves there.

But, my Lords, conditions in Arabia have been changing and, as the noble Lord has said, the new wealth has undermined many of the ancient and respectable traditions. Western goods, Cadillacs and canned foods, refrigerators and radios, and Western ideas (which also come in cans, in the form of films) have undermined the old sanction of Koranic law, and sanctions of morality have crumbled. Vice is unrestrained and the means to gratify unusual lusts can easily be procured with money. There are now sheikhs who can obtain sexual satisfaction only with very young children.

Slaves are often horribly abused for pleasure or mutilated as a punishment, and the castration of young boys is practised. The operation is performed on boys between the ages of ten and fourteen, and the amputation is done radically, both the penis and the scrotum being cut away.

My Lords, the children in shackles in the Buraimi Oasis were destined for Riyadh. The boys might be castrated and the girls bought by any merchant who fancied them. One of the British representatives there, in the Buraimi Oasis, noticed caravans and lorries coming into a little village called Hamasso at night, and when he tried to visit the houses he was denied admittance. So he began to watch the departure of Saudi aeroplanes. I should say that the planes were all Dakotas and, with the exception of one pilot, all the air crews were American. Shortly before the take-off a lorry would drive on to the airstrip and the children would be literally pushed and herded into the plane. My friend (I am sorry to have to keep saying "my friend" but he does not want his name used) then spoke to one of the American pilots and asked him into his house for a drink. He said to him, "Do you realise that you are carrying children into captivity?" And the man answered, "When I took on this job I was told to keep my eyes shut and my ears shut as to what was going on around here. And that is the way it is going to be. Another seven years of flying for King Saud and I'll have earned enough money to retire for life."

This information, in point of fact, I happen to know, was reported to the Foreign Office. It was never used at the time of the Buraimi frontier dispute, nor since. Why? Because the Foreign Office do not wish to embarrass a powerful Ally. Nor, I may say, is it only the Foreign Office who do not want to embarrass a powerful Ally. When I tried to interest various editors in this matter, some of these steely-eyed despots were alarmed at the matter which they thought might be revealed by my inquiries. The very steel of their eyes grew tarnished at the prospect. However, at last I found an editor who was prepared to back me. I then found that I was given no visas to enter any of the countries on the Trucial Coast. But since I could not get into the Coast and could not get into Saudi Arabia, I decided to examine the alternative route. And last year I travelled in a Land Rover from Gambia, through Senegal and Mauritania, into what was then the French Sudan and to the legendary city of Timbuktu, where I lived for a month making various inquiries. I then moved out into the Sahara. And there I bought a slave from his Tuareg master, like one buys a piece of meat. I paid for him 25,000 A.O.F. francs, which is the equivalent of £37 10s. His name was Ibrahim. He was twenty years old. I gave him his freedom and he now works as a free man in Timbuktu. My Lords, I bought this man and photographed the money changing hands with the master and took the number of the notes and so forth, entirely in order to come back with the actual proof that slavery exists in the Sahara.

The Tuareg are nomadic tribesmen, fair skinned, who have a slave caste known as the Bela. These Bela, men, women and children, belong to their masters body and soul. I have lived in these Tuareg camps, and I have seen these slave girls and slave women working from dawn until dusk. I should explain that among the Tuareg women fatness is considered a sign of great beauty, and so the Tuareg women are not allowed to do any work, even if they want to. So there they lay, rather like sealions in the zoo after feeding time, watching their slaves from behind the folds of their indigo veils, and doing nothing. Moreover, the Tuareg caste of nobles refer to and think of themselves as nobles; and nobles do no work—nobles in the Sahara, I mean to say! No Tuareg noble would think of handling a spade, erecting a tent or carrying a gourd of water. And so they have these great herds of slaves, exactly as they have always had great herds of sheep; and in the great wastes of the Sahara they have been able to preserve this institution of slavery some 65 years after the French occupation put an end to slavery.

I have lived in these camps and seen these little skinny boys, with bellies horribly distended from malnutrition, going out in the morning, before dawn, with the herds; and I have known that, until they came back in the evening, they would be in the desert without anything to eat or drink. And when they got back, after the Tuareg nobles had eaten, and after their wives had had their ration of milk, if there was anything left they would get it. I have seen the marks of cruelty on their bodies. If they are disobedient, or if they lose an animal by neglect, they are tied to a tree and lashed until they lose consciousness—and sometimes they do not recover and are just left to die.

I have met, and know well, a little girl—Timulud is her name —who is sixteen years old. At the age of eleven, she was raped by her master. She has already had two children. The first was still-born, and the second was left behind when they moved camp because it was sick; and they told her to leave it in the desert. Long before these girls reach maturity, they are used by their masters; and if, as a result of rape, a child is born, that child is born a slave unless the master happens to wish, by some quirk of his own, to acknowledge it; but that happens very seldom. So when I gave Ibrahim his freedom, it meant not only that he could escape from the persecution of his master, and not only, as your Lordships have heard the noble Lord say, that his master could take him to Mecca with him on a pilgrimage (and I have met a sheikh who went to Mecca with six children and returned with none because he had sold them all, like a human traveller's cheque) but also that he could marry the girl he loved and that the children of that union would be born free.

My Lords, slavery exists throughout West Africa, concealed behind a legal code that asserts it has been abolished, like a cancer the doctors refuse to diagnose. French and British authorities are trying hard, and have tried hard, to stamp out slavery in the areas that are under their control. But as these African countries, one by one, gain their independence, they are going to be forced to deal with the problems themselves. Now I believe that in West Africa, certainly, the problem is largely, or certainly partly, one of education—that is to say, the Tuareg noble has been brought up to believe that the Bela is his slave, and the Bela has been brought up to believe that the Tuareg is his master; to such an extent that a Bela slave who has left the camp but is still working in Timbuktu, when he has made enough money, will come back and buy his freedom from his master, even though he knows that, from the point of view of the law, he is a free man. So it is a question of education. But can these newly independent countries, such as Mauritania, Mali or Nigeria, afford this mass education? They have neither the money nor the people to do it. One might think that the answer was that the former tutelary Power should provide the experts. That, I think, would be disastrous; because, unfortunately, the tides of nationalism have tinged the peoples of Africa with a deep suspicion of the colonialist Powers. A group of English educational experts would therefore be immediately suspect in Nigeria, and a group of French experts —people well equipped to deal with the psychological problem of the Tuareg and their Bela—would be very suspect in Mali.

My Lords, what is the solution? I think it can only be, as we have heard from my noble friend Lord Shackleton, through the United Nations. I should like to stress what he has said: that international Conventions are useless unless they have the machinery for supervising their application. An international Convention is a mere piece of paper if no agency exists for translating its terms into action. I believe that there should be a committee of experts to advise the Economic and Social Council of the United Nations on the decisions they should take about slavery each year. The members of this committee—no more than nine or ten— should be of different nationalities, and preferably not of the nationality of the former tutelary Power. They should be chosen for their knowledge of the problems concerned, and they should be there for an indefinite period to ensure continuity. They would be only advisory: the final decisions would still rest with the Economic and Social Council.

Lastly, I believe that every one of the experts and technicians and advisers needed by African countries should be sent to them by the United Nations. These people should be international not only in outlook but in fact—white or black, red, yellow or brown —and they should go to the Africans as friends, not as patrons. Because, in the final analysis, to the Africans as well as to the Arabs, policies are less important than personalities; and, deep down, political equality is less important than social equality and friendship.

5.57 p.m.

LORD BIRDWOOD: My Lords, we have had quite a time to wait for a maiden speech from the noble Viscount, Lord Maugham, but I think our patience has been rewarded by what might be considered as a very notable contribution—notable, perhaps, because we have discovered one who takes the trouble to go out and see things for himself. In considering a great human problem such as slavery, the number of people in this country who can claim personal experience could be counted on the fingers of one hand; and all the more, then, are we lucky to have had Lord Maugham's eloquence and sincerity to support that personal experience and personal contact with conditions. In the midst of so many grave international situations, the chances to discuss this persistent scourge are few—because, as it seems, the problem is always with us. I find it rather a curious reflection on our interpretation of values to note that this afternoon a very important matter such as the road operations in the Perivale area of the Western Avenue was considered by a full House, whereas the evidence we have just heard was noted by a comparatively scarce House.

We live today with a studied campaign of vilification against Western Powers, accompanied as it is by a ceaseless barrage on the theme of colonialism; and a debate such as the noble Lord, Lord Shackleton, has initiated tends, in my view, to restore our sense of balance and proportion in international affairs. For that reason it is extremely valuable. It helps to remind this House—and, through this House, the public outside that may be interested—that some of those whom we have heard most effective and most noisy in the campaign to which I have referred are themselves responsible for conditions so barbaric as should, in a world which should be governed by justice, challenge the whole question of their fitness for international status and nationhood—a question which the noble Viscount, Lord Astor, posed this afternoon. We have heard something about the technique in Saudi Arabia. Last year, in the United Nations, some of us had to endure tedious hours of exaggerated oratory from the distinguished representative of Saudi Arabia, and a constant arraignment of the Western Powers for their alleged crimes, political and humanitarian. Even more pointed did I find the circumstances which enabled a Power such as the Yemen to pontificate on the rights of the child. In October last year, the Third Committee spent several days trying to discover exactly when the rights of a child began. It is a topsy-turvy sort of world when representatives of a country which publicly displays its manacled prisoners chained together and where by no stretch of the imagination do adult men and women receive any rights whatsoever, are able to be taken seriously when they give their opinion on whether the rights of a child begin before or after birth.

We have to make a clear distinction between countries where slavery flourishes by consent, where authority chooses to look the other way, and where it is recognised by statutory arrangement, and other countries where slavery still persists, such as in Nigeria, but where the Administration are fully conscious of their duty in the matter and are doing their best to get on top of the problem. The latter deserve international sympathy and co-operation. The former deserve nothing better than organised international indignation. Even so, that indignation could yield to sympathy if we could be sure that the crime was recognised and that the country concerned was trying to set its house in order.

In referring to organised international indignation, I am throwing the whole weight of anything I can say in support of the noble Lord, Lord Shackleton, for the developing of effective international machinery to deal with this crime. Only in this way can this running sore in the body of international society be healed. We have had our attention drawn to the need to include certain manifestations of slavery which hitherto have not been regarded as slavery within the terms of the 1926 Convention, and as a result we had the Supplementary Convention of September, 1956, which recognised practices similar to slavery as deserving legitimate inquiry. It is within this context that I think it appropriate merely to note that the present Slavery Convention was drafted by a commission of ten which included the Soviet Union.

I know that this is not the right time to spell out the long and tragic story of slave conditions behind the Iron Curtain. There will be other occasions for that. But, on the other hand, I think it would be quite unintelligent that we should neglect those conditions entirely; that we should neglect the fact that the Power which actually contributed to the drafting of the Convention has been responsible for a vast network of slave camps and has been responsible for mass deportations from Hungary, the three liquidated Baltic States and Ruthenia. If anybody doubts the matter, they can study a publication of a perfectly respectable international organisation, the International Confederation of Free Trade Unions, which has gone into the whole business. Where physical slavery has played itself out, so to speak, there mental slavery has taken over. The methods of operation may be those of mass production in contrast to private enterprise, as obtains in the Middle East, but the results are equally devastating. I repeat; if there is to be an international conscience in this matter, it is impossible that those conditions should be passed over—certainly not by any international machinery that is set up.

It is on the assumption that we have an international conscience in this matter that one asks whether the machine can be strengthened so as to make it more effective. In the last report of the Anti-Slavery Society, last month, the Director insisted (I think the noble Lord, Lord Shackleton, referred to this) that while the Convention looks well enough on paper it is meaningless in its implementation. One sentence from the report, I think, is sufficient to bring home this point:

"None of the States concerned, which are under an obligation to furnish the United Nations with information under Article 7 of the Slavery Convention of 1956, have done so and it is nobody's business to remind them of their obligation."

This, I suggest, indicates future conditions. The Director's solution is the appointment of either a small expert committee of three to five members—the noble Viscount, Lord Maugham, mentioned ten—or a single expert. The function would be to sit at the elbow of the Economic and Social Council, receive reports and information, interpret them, advise generally and operate as an expert pressure group in the international sense. I find this extremely sensible, but I want to suggest an extension of its function.

To drive home my point I shall have to make a diversion for a moment. Your Lordships will recall that under the trusteeship system those responsible for trustee territories have to receive every three years, a mission from the United Nations, which reports to the Trusteeship Council. In this way, we ourselves have received United Nations visitors in Togoland, the Cameroon and Tanganyika, and I think that on the whole we have managed to satisfy them. Surely it is equally rational that a similar system of inspection should be introduced by the Economic and Social Council in attempting to get on top of this problem of slavery. Why should the administrative achievement of a district officer in Tanganyika be a matter for international concern and inquiry while barbaric practices committed by Africans in Timbuktu are exempt?

I rather suspect that the answer one might receive in putting forward this kind of proposal would be that if the representatives of the United Kingdom tabled a resolution in the Third Committee, they would not receive in terms of votes sufficient support to pass the resolution. I shall always be extremely unsympathetic to that kind of suggestion. If we agree that the machinery needs strengthening, surely it is our duty to put up measures which we believe would be effective for the purpose. The fact that the measures may not be accepted in no way exonerates us from our duty of putting them forward. One wonders how much would ever be achieved if everybody started counting heads before they put forward one sane and just proposal. The only man who dislikes the police court is the man who stands his trial. The only man who dislikes the customs office is the smuggler.

It may be of some interest and it might serve an international purpose, in my view, to know exactly who would support and who would resist the proposal for a small international team of experts charged with the duty of inspection on the spot where slavery is concerned. I should have thought that the modern generation of a land which gave birth to a Wilberforce and a Lugard would expect Her Majesty's Government to put pressure on the international organisation and exert positive leadership in supporting a measure which could go a long way to end slavery for all time.

6.10 p.m.

LORD AMULREE: My Lords, I want to say a few words in support of this suggestion put forward by the noble Lord, Lord Shackleton. Until I came here today my sole knowledge of what was going on in the slave traffic derived from what I have read in the Reports of the Anti-Slavery Society. But now we have had an extraordinarily vivid story told by the noble Viscount, Lord Maugham—and I should like to join in congratulating him upon a remarkable maiden speech containing a great deal of information on this matter which he has given to your Lordships —which confirms what one had read and what one thought, and shows how necessary it is for some such action as that suggested by the noble Lord, Lord Shackleton, to be taken.

There are really horrifying stories of what goes on in the Arabian countries, and whether news of these conditions has been kept from us for commercial and economic reasons I do not know, but now we have been told what they are. They are shocking and frightening. One has heard of the tale of children being used as personal traveller's cheques by these wealthy sheikhs going on their pilgrimages; but now that it is confirmed by other noble Lords one sees that there is a great deal of truth behind these stories. What is even more frightening is that one realises that this traffic involves countries with which we are intimately connected. I know it is not their fault and they do their best to put down the traffic when it occurs, but that it should occur there at all shows how widespread it all is.

It was in December, 1949, when your Lordships were discussing a Bill to make a new planning of Parliament Square and there was a great amount of discussion about the Buxton Memorial Fountain which stood at the corner of George Street. We debated this fountain for some four of five hours because it was the one memorial put up in London to the anti-slavery movement. A great deal was then said by noble Lords about the great work Great Britain had done in the past to bring about the abolition of slavery in the world. I feel that your Lordships have given a very good follow-up from that debate to the debate that we are now having, and this shows that we still retain our great interest in the abolition of this appalling traffic.

It has been said by many people—but by nobody here, I am thankful to say—that the lot of the slave is not a bad one and he is far more comfortably taken care of than he would be if he were free, living in his own country. The same has been said sometimes about these countries that are now emerging from a state of benevolent paternalism under other countries. But it just is not true. People would far rather be free, even though not so well fed, so well housed or so well taken care of. Therefore I want to give all the support I can to the noble Lord who has put down this Question, and I trust that we shall get a satisfactory reply from the noble Marquess.

6.15 p.m.

LORD FARINGDON: My Lords, before I say one or two words on this Question, I take great pleasure in felicitating my noble friend Lord Maugham on a truly admirable and impressive maiden speech, both in form and in context: indeed, I would pay him the highest compliment in saying that it was the kind of speech that one would expect to hear from the bearer of his name. I rise only to say a few words and to draw attention to a problem which is a domestic one. Most of the instances which have been quoted to us this afternoon have concerned territories which are directly beyond our control, but there is one part within the frontiers of the Commonwealth where slavery, at any rate, until quite recently, did exist. I refer to the deplorable traffic in slaves up and down the coast river in Eastern Nigeria. I hope that when the noble Marquess comes to reply he may be able to tell me that that trade no longer exists, but only a few years ago I was assured that the trade in boys who were taken up the river and sold to farmers in French territory, and in girls who were taken down the river and sold to Fernando Po, was very lively and causing great anxiety to the administrators in the area. I was told that the principal exponent was a woman, who I believe is no longer in the territory. This is an example which is very close to us and one for which we are directly responsible, and I hope that when he comes to reply the noble Marquess will be able to assure me that it is already a thing of the past.

6.17 p.m.

THE JOINT PARLIAMENTARY UNDER-SECRETARY OF STATE FOR FOREIGN AFFAIRS (THE MARQUESS OF LANSDOWNE): My Lords, I am sure we are all grateful to the noble Lord, Lord Shackleton, for having put down this Question. I think it is most important that this horrible subject should be ventilated. We have listened to extremely well-informed speeches. I should like to add my word of congratulation to the noble Viscount, Lord Maugham, on a remarkably well-informed and thought-out maiden speech. I would, however, at the outset of my remarks join issue with the noble Viscount when he says that he has the impression that the Foreign Office do not believe what is true—that was what I took him to be saying. Let me at once assure the noble Viscount that here he fell into error. We wish naturally to be the masters of the true facts but, as I am sure he will be the first to appreciate, they are not easily come by; and we are, of course, grateful to the noble Viscount for the trouble to which he has gone to obtain factual information on this very distressing subject.

As the noble Lord, Lord Shackleton, who put down the

Question said, we in this country, ever since the time of Wilberforce, have been in the lead in our efforts to obtain freedom for the individual. I can assure the noble Viscount that we feel as strongly now as ever we did. It was, as I know the noble Lord is fully aware, due to us that the 1956 Supplementary Slavery Convention was adopted, and there are thirty-five parties to it now. Her Majesty's Government, of course, consider, as I am sure do all noble Lords, that slavery in any form, whether the slave may be deemed to be more comfortable than he could perhaps be if he were free, is a degrading and terrible thing. But we have to bear in mind—and I was glad to hear this come out in the course of the remarks made by various noble Lords who have spoken—that it is largely a question of education that is going to be required so that the international conscience, to which the noble Lord, Lord Birdwood, referred, will be felt by all concerned.

In his original Question the noble Lord, Lord Shackleton, asked what information was available to Her Majesty's Government on this question of the continued existence of slavery. As I have already said to the noble Viscount, it is difficult to get accurate official information. As was pointed out, where there is profit there will be risks taken; and as you have the sale of narcotics and noxious drugs and so on, so there exists—and we do not deny this—also slavery. If there is sufficient profit in it, alas! this terrible trade may continue covertly however hard we all may try to uncover it.

Nevertheless, I think there are certain reasons for a degree of optimism. As your Lordships know, there have been reports of increasing numbers of prosecutions for slavery, for instance in the Nigerian courts. I do not think that that necessarily means that slavery itself is on the increase. I think it would probably be true to say that these increasing prosecutions have been brought about by a change of heart and a change of attitude. I think that the authorities have been more successful in their efforts because the public at large is more ready to report cases of slavery. So, in reply to the noble Lord, Lord Faringdon (though I do not pretend for a moment that the circumstances to which he referred in Eastern Nigeria no longer exist), I would say that there is a better climate of opinion, and that there is every likelihood that this terrible situation to which he referred, and of which I have some personal knowledge, having lived in French Equatorial Africa for some time, will be gradually improved. But I would not pretend for a moment that I believe it has entirely disappeared.

Under the Convention, one of the obligations of the signatories is that the parties should undertake to communicate to the Secretary General of the United Nations copies of any laws, regulations or administrative measures enacted or put into effect to implement the provisions of the Convention, and to give information of what is going on. As the noble Lord, Lord Shackleton, reminded us, it is a regrettable fact but, alas! true, that only the United Kingdom has fulfilled this obligation. We do not believe that this instrument is perfect. I think that the observations made by the various speakers today should be seriously considered. I perfectly well appreciate that a Convention which, as it were, has no "teeth" in it, may risk being ineffective. But we have to consider that it is quite possible we should not have achieved this supplementary Convention of 1956 at all if the establishment of a supervisory organisation had been insisted upon, because of the risk, as it might have seemed, of intervention in matters which are essentially within the domestic jurisdiction of any State—the old argument with which we are all so familiar. But, we have to take life as it is, and it is quite possible that had these suggestions which have been made today been insisted upon in 1956, we might not have achieved a Convention at all.

I should like to say this to the noble Lord, Lord Shackleton, on what occurred on July 12 in Geneva in the Social Committee. Our representative had instructions to raise this question of slavery at the meeting of the Economic and Social Council, and it is perfectly correct that in fact the question was raised first by Denmark. But I do not think the noble Lord should take us too much to task for that. It happened that Denmark spoke first. The representative of the United Kingdom spoke strongly in support, and was, in fact, the only other speaker. So the noble Lord, Lord Shackleton, should not chide us too much over not having taken the initiative. The instructions were given, and it so happened that Denmark rose to speak first.

I am not going to commit Her Majesty's Government from this Despatch Box this evening to any dramatic change in our policy, but I can asssure your Lordships that what has been said here will be carefully noted. I am quite certain that if the Secretary General of the United Nations should report that he considers it necessary that there should be consultants, some sort of special committee, to advise him on matters arising out of the implementation of the 1956 Convention and, in particular, out of reports that have been furnished by the signatory States, Her Majesty's Government would give such a proposal serious consideration. I cannot go further than that this evening.

I should like to thank noble Lords who have spoken, and I should like to repeat my thanks to the noble Lord, Lord Shackleton. I do not suppose for one moment that he will be satisfied with what I have said, but I can assure him that careful note is being taken. I believe he knows full well that what has been achieved already has taken time. What is still left to be done will also take time. But there is no question of an ostrich-like approach by Her Majesty's Government to this problem. We do not wish to conceal from ourselves the facts, and certainly we shall continue in the same way as ever to do everything we can to ensure the freedom of the individual which, after all, is one of the basic principles of our ideals.

LORD SHACKLETON: My Lords, while I have no right to reply, may I ask the noble Marquess a supplementary question? As he said, he did not expect me to be satisfied, although we are always charmed by his replies. In view of the really brilliant speech of my noble friend Lord Maugham, and the evidence which has been put forward, and in view of the noble Marquess's own statement, that we should take life as we find it, would he not consider stimulating the Secretary General of the United Nations, and indeed finding out whether he regards himself as empowered to ask for the setting up of such a committee without a further Motion? I do not want to make a speech. Again I pay tribute to what was done in 1956. What we are asking is what further steps the Government might take, and whether they could take those through the Secretary General.

THE MARQUESS OF LANSDOWNE: My Lords, the noble Lord is probably right in saying that he was breaking the rules, but never mind. I am unable to give a straight reply to that question, but I repeat what I said already: that I have taken very careful note of what the noble Lord has said. I can go no further.

BIBLIOGRAPHY

Ancient and Modern Slavery—C. S. Taylor
Slavery in the Twentieth Century—Lewis
Black Ivory and White—Zubair Ibn Rahmata Pasha
Slavery—Lady Simon
The Arab at Home—Dr. Paul Harrison
Doctor in Arabia—Dr. Paul Harrison
Holy Cities of Arabia—Eldon Rutter
Slavery Through the Ages—Sir George McMunn
Islam on Slavery—Lord Headley (Pamphlet)
Mohammedanism—Professor Snouck Hurgronje
Secrets of the Black Sea—Henry de Monfried
Voyage to the Congo—André Gide
Slave Markets—Joseph Kessel
The Government of Ethiopia—Margery Perham
Ethiopia under Haile Selassie—Mrs. C. Sandford
The Influence of Islam—Rev. E. J. Bolus
What is Slavery?—Nina Boyle (Pamphlet)
A French Doctor in the Yemen—Dr. Claudie Fayein
Sand Kings of Oman—Raymond O'Shea
The Arabs of the Desert—Dickson
Arabian Journey—Colonel Gerald de Gaury
Slavery—C. W. W. Greenidge
The Slaves of Timbuktu—Robin Maugham